MEDITATIONS
BY THE SEA

Delia Halverson

Meditations
BY THE
Sea

Northstone

Editors: Michael Schwartzentruber, Dianne Greenslade
Cover design: Margaret Kyle
Interior design: Julie Bachewich
Shell art: from the public domain
Consulting art director: Robert MacDonald

Northstone Publishing acknowledges the financial support of the
Government of Canada through the Book Publishing Industry
Development Program for its publishing activities.

Northstone Publishing is an imprint of Wood Lake Books Inc., an
employee-owned company, and is committed to caring for the
environment and all creation. Northstone recycles, reuses, and
composts, and encourages readers to do the same. Resources are
printed on recycled paper and more environmentally friendly
groundwood papers (newsprint), whenever possible. The trees used
are replaced through donations to the Scoutrees for Canada program.
Ten percent of all profit is donated to charitable organizations.

Canadian Cataloguing in Publication Data
Halverson, Delia Touchton
Meditations by the Sea
ISBN 1–896836–30–5
1. Meditations. I. Title.
BV4832.2.H24 1999 242 C98–911206–3

Published by Northstone Publishing,
an imprint of Wood Lake Books Inc.
Kelowna, British Columbia, Canada

Printing 10 9 8 7 6 5 4 3 2 1
Printed in Canada by
Transcontinental Printing and Graphics Inc.

To those who share the joy of the seashore,
whether it be a small inland sea
or a vast ocean.
To those of the past
who have given us wisdom from the sea,
whether they realized it as a gift
or simply shared their own joy.

Contents

~ Introduction

Although I lived within 40 miles of the Gulf of Mexico as a child, the visits to the sea were always special occasions. They were never as frequent as I would have liked, and they never lasted long enough. But they were the source for a store of memories that have lasted a lifetime. Numerous trips to other beaches, some similar to my childhood beaches and many far different, have increased that memory log.

Each seashore has its own unique beauty, and each has its own way of drawing us to our Creator. But unless we take the time to look for that uniqueness and the beauty that it brings, we will view the sea with blinders. We will only see what we expect to see.

I hope that some of these reflections will help you to remove the blinders and will draw you closer to God, as the hours spent writing this book have done for me. Each time I look out over the sea I gain a new perspective. Likewise, it is interesting how in my conversations with people who actually live day in and day out with a constant view of the sea, I've found them still awed and excited over their contact with the sea. They may not spend long hours actually roaming the shores, but they continue to be renewed by its presence and power.

Perhaps the mystery that still surrounds the sea is a part of this. We cannot know all that is happening under the surface of the water. And so people return to the sea again and again. For without mystery in our life we become complacent.

If the sea is a mystery, God is the greatest mystery of all. If we knew all that there is to know about God, then God would not be God. The unknowable but yet all-loving aspects of God are what continue to draw us closer to our Creator.

Adam and Eve found God in the unknown of a tree in the Garden. Noah found God in the unknown of a seemingly endless rain.

Moses found God in the unknown of a living bush on fire. David found God in the unknown of forgiveness when he repented. And Jesus exhibited God in the unknown ability to love, even in the face of his enemies.

We may never solve all the mysteries of the sea, but we can take those mysteries, along with our basic knowledge, and use them to search out the character of God. I hope that this book does a bit of that.

Low Tides
When Spirits Are Low

Tides rise and fall with regularity. We know that a high tide will follow the low tide. Although our spirits are not as predictable as tides, we can find help in the times of our low spirits.

~ of sunsets and moonrises

There are very few beaches where one is privileged to watch both the sunset and the moonrise. An island that stretches from east to west allows this unusual occurrence.

All too often, we equate the sunset with an ending. We speak of old age as "living in the sunset of our lives" or we call a day "from sunrise to sunset." Because it is dark after sunset, and because we often fear what we cannot see, we associate darkness with fear. However, without darkness we cannot appreciate light.

Persons who have gone through the darkness of a great crisis tell us how much they appreciate the peace that they have found after the crisis. Often the crisis creates a much stronger character. And it can certainly strengthen our relationship with God. However, I cannot believe that God creates the crisis in order to firm that relationship.

I believe that God desires for us all to live happy and fruitful lives, without crises, and to grow in our relationship with God. But God has also given us free will, and sometimes we, or someone else, choose some action that creates a crisis for ourselves or another person. God has also set up laws in the universe, and some of those laws we are just beginning to understand. At times of pain and trauma, I believe God *shares* in our sorrow and trauma.

Out of these circumstances, however, God can bring about a deeper faith, if we allow it to happen. Into the darkness, the moon will rise.

You created the moon
to tell us the seasons.
The sun knows when to set,
and you made the darkness...

Psalm 104:19–20a (all quotations CEV, unless otherwise noted)

I pray, O God, for the peace
you can give during the
fearful "nights" of my life.
As the biblical Hebrew day actually began
at sunset,
let the darkness and moonrise
become a new day
in my relationship with you. Amen.

~ of boulders and bluffs

It was a great day for walking the beach. The tide was low, with a broad ribbon of sand between the water on one side and the boulders and bluffs on the other. I rolled up the legs of my pants and began scuffing along in the shallow water, looking for shells. Unmindful of the time, I collected handfuls of the delightful mollusks, being careful to throw back any that were alive.

Eventually I recognized that time had slipped away from me, and so I turned to retrace my steps. Suddenly I was confronted with a dilemma. Once I had walked into the sea, I had paid no attention to my surroundings. Now, in front of me, a boulder jutted out into the sea. I did not even recall seeing it when I had walked down the beach. The tide had come in as I had mindlessly walked the sands. Now the water was too deep to wade through, and if I carried my prized shells I certainly could not swim around the boulder. Even if I tried, I was fearful that the waves would knock me against the rocks. And so the only other choice I had was to find a place where I could climb up the bank and walk around the boulder. I felt hemmed in, surrounded by obstacles. How had I let this happen to me?

Sometimes we feel as if all of life surrounds us like boulders, too high to climb over and too dangerous to swim around. This seems particularly true in today's busy world. However, we can be assured that we are not the first people to feel this way. Adam and Eve may have seen the tree of knowledge as an obstacle, Moses dealt with his speech impediment, and certainly the psalmists experienced many trials.

Despite all of the times that we read of obstacles in the Bible, we find rocks referred to as a positive metaphor throughout it. We read of God being our rock, our solid foundation when things get rough. At least 10 percent of the Psalms refer to God as a rock, and Jesus spoke of building a house on a rock instead of the sand.

As I look at the boulders on the beach, I realize that winds and waters beat on the shores every day, sometimes with a great fury. Hurricanes may come and go, leaving trees uprooted and beach homes in shambles. Fire can sweep down the beach and rain can cause mud slides, but these large boulders will remain. They are steady. They are dependable. They are forever there. There is much truth in the Bible's metaphor of God, our steady and dependable rock, our stronghold through it all.

You, LORD God, are my fortress,
that mighty rock where I am safe.

Psalm 94:22

My God, you are like a mighty rock,
standing with me against the winds
and battering waves.
I thank you for being there,
ready and unwavering. Amen.

~ of reefs in the sea

With the wind in my face, I sat in the bow of the boat, anticipating the end of the ride and the opportunity to slip overboard into the crystal waters. I checked my snorkel mask again. The last time I had tried this had been a miserable experience because my mask had not fit. This time I made sure I had a good fit so that it would not leak water.

Finally we arrived at the reef, and I eased into the water. I stretched out on the water, and the mask held tight. Now I could relax, allowing the water to hold me up as I observed the miracle of life below.

Soon I was caught up in the drama below the surface of the water. Before me every color of fish made a rainbow of movement. As I viewed the gigantic kaleidoscope, I thanked God for making the world in color. I would never have experienced the full joy of sight had the world been made in black and white.

Finally my attention moved from the big picture, and I watched the interplay of fish. Some fish fed on grasses and some foraged in the sand for small sea creatures. A sergeant major caught my eye as it emerged from the grass. Suddenly it darted into a crack in the coral. As I looked around I saw a yellowtail snapper swim into the area, causing the fish to scatter. The sergeant major was safely hidden in the crack in the reef.

I was reminded of the biblical references to God as our refuge. The coral reef provides a protective refuge for the sergeant major. And just as the reef stands firm, ready to accept and protect the fish, God is always available as our shelter from that which may destroy us.

Then I thought about how we have ruined so many coral reefs during the past century. We have ruined the reef by stripping it bare; we have ruined it by dragging boats across it; we have ruined it by killing it with pollution. How often do we also ruin our opportunities

to accept God's refuge. We place barriers between ourselves and God; we lose our direction; we cloud up the situation with unclean
thoughts so that we cannot even see God
around us.

We must clear our path to God. We must
make a habit of turning to God for help without hesitancy or uncertainty.

Please listen, God,
and answer my prayer!
I feel hopeless, and I cry out to you
from a faraway land.
Lead me to the mighty rock
high above me.

Psalm 61:1–2

My God, help me to
keep you ever before me,
knowing that your protection
is always there whether I see it or not.
Help me to recognize
your protective presence
and to share
that safe sanctuary with others.
Amen.

~ of that strange bird, the pelican!

The pelican is a rather strange bird, with its bucket-sized beak. As a child I often heard the little rhyme, "A funny bird is the pelican. Its beak can hold more than its belly can." The pelican *is* a funny bird when walking, and it appears to be unbalanced when standing still. From the beach, pelicans cannot see into the waters to find fish for a meal.

But watch the pelican in flight! It will swoop from above and coast along, making absolutely no obvious wing movement. Catching the current of the wind, the pelican seems to effortlessly rest in midair while going about the daily work of catching fish.

Sometimes I feel awkward and inept at what I'm doing. I feel sort of like a bird that's too big for its short legs, wobbling along the shore, unable to see my goal. Everywhere I turn there are graceful, long-legged birds delicately stepping through the tide and coming up with an abundance of fish.

I forget that God has made us all unique, each with his or her own gifts. I may have to wobble along the shore from time to time when something must be done, especially if that particular activity or mission isn't my special gift. But there are also times when I can soar with the wind, times when my true gifts take flight and I am lifted up on God's air currents. From the vantage point of my own gifts and talents, I can easily see my goal and I am lifted on the currents of God's love to go about reaching it. But I must discover my gifts and make use of them.

Like the baby pelican, I must venture out of the nest and try my own wings, trusting God's wisdom in placing the particular gifts within me. I will find my strength in the Lord, who made the heavens and the earth, the land and the sea, and placed special gifts within me.

But those who trust in the LORD
will find new strength.
They will be strong like eagles
soaring upward on wings;
they will walk and run
without getting tired.

Isaiah 40:31

I pray, Oh Lord,
for the courage to trust you,
for the insight to find my gifts,
and for the joy of being lifted up
on your wind currents! Amen.

~ of shells and roots

Often when I walk the beaches I think of those who came before me. In recent decades, most likely these shores were filled with people who spent hot summer afternoons enjoying a picnic and the cool breezes, or with fishermen with their nets, casting for fish. But what sort of peoples inhabited the beaches a thousand years ago? Did they love and laugh like I do? Did they mourn over lost loved ones? Did they fear that their homes would be destroyed? Were they wandering folk, or did they live settled lives in houses?

When I pick up a large shell, I reflect on just how such a shell might have been used in an earlier community. Archeologists tell us that shells were commonly used as utensils and ceremonial containers in earlier coastal communities. A family that was different, but yet very much like mine, could have used this type of shell as a scoop. Or it might have been used to hold water. Perhaps such a shell held ceremonial oils used in the ritual union of a man and a woman.

We have deeper roots than history books reveal. We not only trace our heritage through our genealogical roots, but also through our sociological and religious roots. People of the past, all over the world, used their creative energies to improve their way of living. They styled utensils from wood and clay and shells; they developed tools of stone and wood, shells and metals. They domesticated animals to expand their production. And they passed the knowledge on, each generation improving the work of the ones before them.

Our religious roots also reach back through the ages. And it is surprising how that heritage parallels our scientific heritage. Our early understandings of God have changed as we have gained new understandings of our world that God made. We no longer believe that God sends disasters to punish or to teach. We have learned that all people are equal in God's eyes, and we recognize God as a God for all peoples.

We trace our religious roots back to early church leaders, to Paul and the original disciples, to the kings and prophets, to Moses and Abraham, to before recorded history. For God placed in us the very heart of desire for that growing relationship with God.

When I am low in spirits, it helps me to pick up a shell and remember my baptism into the family of God, and also to remember the roots of my religious heritage.

God blesses those people who depend only on [God]. They belong to the kingdom of heaven!

Matthew 5:3

There are times, Lord,
when I feel very much like
the poor in spirit that Jesus referred
to in the Beatitudes.
Those are the times
when I must remember my baptism
and remember my roots. Amen.

~ of rocks and water

Some folks think "the seashore is the seashore is the seashore." They recognize no variety in the scenery. But if you have a true interest in the sea, you will discover great variety. Where the earth is flat and sandy you will find a broad beach with dunes and grasses (unless people have destroyed the natural dunes). But where the earth is hilly and steep, rocks litter the shore and protrude into the sea.

It was on such a rocky beach that I walked with friends one day. Rather than looking at the sea, we turned our attention to the rocks. Some rocks had no distinguishing shape, but others seemed to resemble an animal or some object. We found rocks that looked like turtles, rocks that looked like a cityscape, and even a rock that looked like the head of my friends' dog which had recently died. Although the shapes of the rocks intrigued me, it was what caused the rocks to take on such shapes that ultimately drew my interest.

The water had tossed about the individual rocks piled along the shore. Many were worn smooth; some so smooth that when they were wet they looked like large, polished, semiprecious stones. Yet the rocks were heavy and so solid that I don't believe I could have broken them with a sledgehammer. It was not a single blow that shaped and smoothed those rocks. In fact, a single blow would have left jagged edges, harmful to those who touched them. It was the constant, regular movement of water that caused the rocks to shine and glow and to become smooth to the touch.

I thought, we are much like that. When someone criticizes us or commands us with a single blow, our sharp edges may become exposed. We are very likely to hurt someone, intentionally or otherwise. But when the water of love washes over us regularly, constantly, then we become like semiprecious stones, shining with that love that first came from God.

We are more interlaced with God's plan than we often recognize. Too often we try to conquer nature, instead of using God's design in nature as our guide. We want to take control instead of allowing God's love to work through us.

In the beginning, LORD,
you laid the earth's foundation
and created the heavens.
They will all disappear
and wear out like clothes.
You change them as you would a coat, but
you last forever.
You are always the same.
Years cannot change you.
Every generation of those who
serve you will live in your presence.

Psalm 102:25–28

God, you are the great architect
of all that is.
Every part of nature is
incorporated into your great "I Am."
Help us to learn from your great design.
Give us patience when
we have the urge to try to transform others
with a single blow,
and make us like constant,
flowing water, shining and
polishing with your love. Amen.

~ of sandy feet
and soul refreshment

There comes a time during every day at the beach when I'm ready to trade my beach shoes for a fresh water shower! By the time I've played in the surf, built sandcastles with a child, and doused myself with several layers of suntan lotion, I begin to feel like a walking sandbox. Add a touch of sunburn and eyes burning from sweat, and a shower sounds luxurious, even if it's only a garden hose!

As I stand under the shower, feeling all the sand and lotion slide from my body, I have two special thoughts. First, I marvel that God created my face in such a way that when I stand under the cascading water I don't drown. If my nose were put on my face the other way around, then the water would easily run into it. Actually, the shape of the nose is so perfectly engineered that I can breathe deeply under the shower and still not draw any water into my lungs.

Then, as I complete my shower and stand refreshed, I recall the psalmist's words and remember my baptism. After a day at the beach, I can really appreciate the symbolism of baptism – washing my spirit clean and preparing me for Christ's service just as water washes me clean and prepares me for the day's work.

No matter what has gone on before, no matter how sandy and grimy my spirit has become, no matter how frustrated I feel, remembering my baptism brings refreshment to my soul. This is especially so when I remember that God chose me and continues to affirm me, even when I slip back into the world's largest sandbox or messiest mudslide! All I have to do is head for the showers!

Wash me with hyssop* until I am clean and
whiter than snow...
Create pure thoughts in me
and make me faithful again.

Psalm 51:7, 10

My God, create in me a clean heart,
and wash the whole of me too. Amen.

* In biblical times, hyssop was used to sprinkle water in a
purifying act.

High Tides
When Spirits Are High

Just as high tides bring interesting treasures from the sea, the high tides of our lives leave us with treasured memories. We need to hold on to the memories of those high tides, for they can be like jewels, shining in the darkness.

~ of down days and new days

It was a new day on the beach. The tide was high, covering the scuff marks and the debris left the previous day. God had washed the world that night with sweet showers from the sky, leaving the grasses and rocks clean of dust and dirt. What a day for a new start!

I breathed in the fresh scent of the sea, stretched my hands to the rising sun, and thanked God for this opportunity to be alive. This was a day to file away in my memory, a redemptive sort of day. When spirits are low we often forget that we've experienced such days. This was the sort of day to store away and pull out of the memory bank when those rough days come about. This was a day I'd use to redeem my spirits in the future when they were low.

When I was a child I learned Psalm 118:24 from the King James Version: "This is the day that the LORD hath made. Let us rejoice and be glad in it." We only recited the verse on Sunday, and consequently I thought that the psalmist had written it only for Sundays, or for the days that we went to church. The verse was usually coupled with the psalmist's verse about entering the house of the Lord: "I was glad when they said unto me, Let us go into the house of the LORD" (Psalm 122:1). Or did I put the verses together simply because these two verses were the only ones I could ever remember?

As an adult, however, I have learned that Psalm 118:24 is appropriate on any day, even my "down" days. It serves to remind me that God has made everything and is in control, even when that control allows us to take command of our own lives and perhaps mess them up. However, since the day does belong to the Lord, then I should use it in service and in communication with God. If I am God's, then every minute of my schedule, whether awake or sleeping, belongs to God. How shall I use it?

This day belongs to the LORD!
Let us celebrate and be glad today.

Psalm 118:24

My God, help me to grasp the day
and recognize that each day is yours. Guide
me in its use so that I
may glorify you in it. Amen.

~ of skimmers and daily bread

Skimmers are such amazing birds. Their bright red and black beaks remind me of a parrot, but their lower beak is longer than the upper. This miraculous arrangement allows the bird to skim food from the water while flying. God's finely tuned universe fits together with a pattern. Some birds make a big splash as they dive deep for fish, while others skim the surface of the water, leaving only a long V on the surface of the water that hardly disturbs the fish.

Many of the birds near the sea nest on poles or masts, or in trees. Skimmers use the warm sand to help incubate their eggs. In order for them to survive in our populated areas, their nesting places must be roped off, protecting their nests from people. I often see them resting together on the white sand, all facing the same direction like tuxedo-dressed groomsmen, waiting for the bride to appear. Although the skimmer doesn't have bright feathers, the vivid black and white coloring demands attention.

Unlike the gulls who dive-bomb each other and appear to swarm when flying together, the skimmers exhibit very synchronized flight patterns and one of the best air shows at the beach! With their wings spread wide, they can rise and fall, and turn in perfect coordination. How much easier life would be for us humans if, like the skimmers, we worked in harmony and with a central goal or purpose.

One seldom sees a skimmer alone, and often they fly in large groups. When they skim along the water scooping up food, they seem to glide for an unusually long time with their wings folded high above their heads, trusting the force of their flight to move them along. Instinctively they know that God provides their food on the surface of the water and that their bodies are designed to help them catch their meal.

If only we could be so trusting in the order of the universe that God created, instead of hoarding food that could be shared with others. As Moses led the people out of Egypt, God provided only that food which was necessary for the people that day. Any food held over spoiled so that it could not be hoarded. In fact, the prayer that Jesus taught us does not say, "Give us all the bread we can eat and extra that we can hoard." It says, "Give us our daily bread." If we take this seriously, we will recognize that we all can be fed with the provisions that God has built into our universe, but we must balance the food among ourselves.

Give us our food for today.

Matthew 6:11

Help us learn from your animals, Lord. We recognize that you created the world in balance. We pray for guidance as we seek to maintain that balance. Amen.

~ of murex shells and priorities

It was a tiny shell, but complete in every ridge, line, and point. Some shells seem to add additional layers as they grow, but the murex begins with nine ridges and the same ridges simply expand and grow larger over time. The small shell that I held in my hand was sprinkled with several tones of brown and beige. But I had already picked up larger murex shells that had less distinctive coloring.

I turned the shell over and found that the organism of the shell had died. This lovely shell produces a foul smelling, yellowish fluid that slowly anesthetizes predators, allowing it to get away. However, when the fluid is exposed to the sun it turns purple. To make a purple dye in Roman times, the soft body parts of the murex were extracted and boiled. It took thousands of shells to produce a tiny amount of dye. This meant that only the very rich or royalty could afford anything that was purple.

Antony and Cleopatra dyed all the sails of their ships purple for the battle of Actium, thereby making a bold statement of their presence.

A color associated with royalty, purple can make one feel privileged to wear it. As an acquaintance of mine said, something that costs a lot of money "makes a statement" of wealth, whether you are wealthy or not.

Antony and Cleopatra boldly announced their presence with purple sails. How do I proclaim my presence? Does that proclamation help others? By my actions, what do I proclaim to be of primary importance to me? Is it money and things, or is it God?

*Only people who don't know God are always
worrying about such things.
Your [God] in heaven knows that you need all
of these. But more than anything else, put
God's work first and do what [God] wants.
Then the other things will be yours as well.*

Matthew 6:32–33

*So often, God, I get my priorities mixed up.
I become anxious for others to know that I
am successful, that I am of great importance.
I fall into the trap of desiring purple cloth
in order to "make a statement."
Let my statement be for others to see
how I love you by my actions. Amen.*

~ of palms and people

I live near the Gulf of Mexico. Visitors often tell me that the palm trees all look the same to them. All they see is a trunk with blades of green matter attached to the top. Those blades of green matter probably provide more cubic inches of equipment for manufacturing oxygen every day of the year than any other type of tree. Palms also provide food, shelter, and clothing for millions of people throughout the tropics. They are considered the most important plants in the world for human survival, next to grasses.

In reality there are thousands of species of palms. They range from a few inches in height to well over 100 feet, with some reaching even 200 feet.

The branches of the palm generally fall into two categories. Some palm branches resemble long feathers, with the fronds draping and swaying in the breeze. Others are more fan-shaped, and indeed have been used as fans. Surprisingly, the palm provides a good bit of shade and is ideally suited to relieve us from the heat. While the tree provides shade, the lower trunk is free of branches, allowing a good circulation of air; this helps to cut down on the mugginess of the summer weather in the tropics. Again, God has provided the right type of tree at the right place.

Along the beach, as I look at the fan-shaped palm branch, I am reminded of the points on a crown. Symbolically, this type of palm stands for kingship, and we use it to recognize the kingship of God over our lives.

But we can also see in the palm frond many individual points coming together at a common center. Each of us in God's kingdom is an individual. The palm branch becomes complete when all fronds are bound together at the base, united into one branch being waved by the wind. *We* are bound together by God's love, and we must work together to create a true kingdom. This palm, which is so typical of the land of Israel, reminds us of the love as well as the kingship of God.

*They shouted, "Blessed is the king who comes
in the name of the LORD!
Peace in heaven and glory to God."*

Luke 19:38

*My God, I look to you as my king in the
midst of my joy as well as in my
sorrow. Bind all of us with your love,
and give us the strength to work
towards the uniting of your kingdom.
Amen.*

~ of geckos and new starts

We were housesitting for a friend, enjoying their lovely home on the beach. We had been in and out of the house several times, moving from the beach to the garden to indoors. As we sat down to relax, a lively gecko darted across the room. It must have been hovering just outside and must have slipped through the opened door. We knew we had to get it outside, and so we began a chase. Each time we thought we had the little reptile cornered, it managed to slip past us. Finally, my husband made a frantic grab. To our exasperation, the gecko dashed off, and we were left holding the tail!

This characteristic is typical of many lizards. And the amazing thing is that they will grow a new tail. The new tail is likely to be a little shorter and to look a little different from the one the lizard lost, but it gives a new beginning for the reptile. Perhaps this is why lizards, which remind us of prehistoric reptiles, have survived for so many years.

We too have opportunities for new starts. In Leviticus, God gives the Hebrews a command for setting up a ten-day period of repentance once a year. This period of repentance is followed by a special day of atonement and forgiveness, called *Yom Kippur*. The Jewish tradition continues to celebrate this special time of atonement, or a time to begin again each fall. In John 8:3–11, we read of the time that Jesus gave a woman a fresh start when he saved her from a death by stoning and told her to go and sin no more. And the celebration of the Eucharist is a time of asking for forgiveness and of turning to lead a new life, an opportunity to start fresh.

As the gecko releases its tail and grows a new one, we also can release our sin and guilt and become new.

Turn your eyes from my sin and cover my guilt. Create pure thoughts in me and make me faithful again.

Psalm 51:9–10

Oh God, my protector, I not only thank you for providing protection, but I thank you for renewing my spirit. Sometimes I find myself hovering around danger, but when I allow danger to snare me, I thank you for the opportunity to renew my commitment and become as new. Amen.

~ of the roar of the ocean

I sat high on the rocks, overlooking the sea. Above me the sky was calming, as the air currents sailed large birds like kites on a string. I lay back on a rock to enjoy the restful sight. Gradually I became aware of a constant sound. It was so constant that I had ignored it earlier. Then I realized I was hearing the roar of the ocean below my rocky ledge. I wondered what the early peoples must have thought caused the roar of the ocean. They had never been far enough to sea to realize that it is quiet away from the breakers.

In biblical times, people believed that God did not exist at sea. The creatures in the sea were unknown, powerful, and some of them larger than life itself. They could not fathom that these creatures were a part of God. That is why Jonah went to sea, to run away from God and the demands that God put upon him. People commonly believed that the roar of the ocean came from sea animals that lived below the surface.

As I listened to the music of the waves hitting against the rocks, I thanked God for new insights, for new understandings of the world. Because I now comprehend the sounds of the ocean, I can join its music with my own joyful praise. I can truly feel at one with the world, lifting my voice in celebration of God's goodness. My next thought is, "How can I share that joy and celebration with others?"

Tell the heavens and the earth to be glad and celebrate! Command the ocean to roar with all of its creatures.

Psalm 96:11

God of the ocean as well as of the earth,
I do desire to praise you.
Help me to use the new insights that come
about each day to praise you
through service to others. Amen.

~ of children playing in the surf

I went to the beach that day to reflect. It was a school day, and there were only a few runners sprinting up and down the beach. I had no more than settled myself with a good book when they hit the sands, a whole busload of school children, laughing and giggling, splashing and digging. Not a single foot was still, and every voice was raised in shouts of laughter. I knew that classes in the area schools typically took a field day to learn about marine biology. This class and I had both chosen the same day to go to the beach, but for different reasons.

I looked at the teacher-chaperone with pity. How could she possibly teach these children anything when there was such chaos? Thankful that it wasn't my job, I turned back to my book, hoping to block the noise from my mind as I became engrossed in what the author had written. After a short time I realized that the laughter and shouts had subsided. I looked up from my book and saw the whole class of children in the surf not far from me. They were gathered around the teacher, and only one captivating voice could be heard – hers. One of the students had found a live cockle, and the calm voice of the teacher was explaining the varying ways that shell creatures move about on and under the ocean floor. The children and I learned that the cockle extends a "foot" out of the space between its shell covering and that it uses it to bury itself in the sand to hide or to search for food. We also learned that the large "foot" of the moon snail inflates with water, becoming twice the size of its shell, which it often covers. The teacher told us that the small slipper shell will attach itself to another shell, relying on the larger shell for its mobility.

As the learning session ended, the children moved back into a playful mood, and I abandoned my book to watch with joy. If only we could all become like children and stop for our "lessons" whenever they come along. But in between, we can release our frustrations in joyful play.

I got up and began wading through the surf myself, feeling the power of the waves as they splashed on my legs, and digging my toes into the sand. God seemed very close to me in that time. I found myself singing an adaptation to a favorite hymn of my mother's, *My God and I Walk through the Fields:*

My God and I play in the surf together.
We laugh with joy as good friends should and do.
God clasps my hands, our voices ring with singing;
My God and I play in the waters blue.

That class of school children taught me a lesson, and I hope I will keep it with me forever. I learned that God created play as well as study. God is not only found in the quiet reflective time, but also in the noisy laughter of children and the roaring splash of the sea.

Praise [God's] name by dancing and playing music on harps and tambourines.

Psalm 149:3

What a joy you created in our play, my Lord. I will try to listen more often and to respond when you call me away to the delight of play. Amen.

~ of the wonder in a child's eyes

The young boy squatted in the sand, intent on something on the edge of the surf. I stood for some time, watching as an expression of awe spread across the child's face. Periodically, he reached his hand out and dug in the sand along the edge of the water. Cautiously I approached the child, being careful not to disturb his thoughts.

As I came closer I saw that the boy was watching some of my favorite shells, the small wedge-shaped coquinas. The shells are also called butterfly shells, because when their halves are spread apart they resemble colorful butterflies. Indeed, they have probably the most varied and colorful designs of any type of shell. Each time the boy dug into the sand, the little wedges popped up straight and seemed to perform a dance as they wiggled their way back into the sand.

Some people would say the boy's expression was one of curiosity. But what might have begun with curiosity now had turned to awe. If it had been only curiosity he would not have continued the same act of digging into the sand and delighting again and again over the joy of color and movement. I saw in that expression recognition of something beyond himself, a bit of wonder and appreciation for the spectacle.

Each time I see this wonder in a child's face, I am convinced that it is a form of worship, a form of appreciation and respect for something greater than the child him- or herself. It is at times like this that I know that children are capable of worship.

Some of the older versions of the Bible use the words fear and awe interchangeably. But they do not mean exactly the same thing. We may fear the atomic bomb, but we are certainly not in awe of it. Awe is a more positive word; fear is more negative.

During creation, God stated that the earth was good. When I remember the day at the beach with that small boy, I stand assured that God is the God of creation, and of goodness.

God looked at what God had done.
All of it was very good!
Genesis 1:31

My God, I see you in a child's face.
I see you in the wonders of the sea.
And I feel you in my heart. I praise you this
day and every day. Amen.

Ebb Tides
Transitional Times

The ebb tide always happens before and after a high tide. It is a time of transition, a time of assessment, a time of new beginnings. When a live shell is washed up on the beach after a high tide, it either digs itself into the wet sand or waits for the next tide to wash it back out to sea. Live shells know how to deal with transitional times.

~ of winds and change

The day began with the click of the radio alarm, and a trusted voice said, "Temperatures today will hover in the low-90s in the inland communities with some possible mid-80s at the beaches, brought about by offshore breezes." The wind on the beaches would make quite a difference in the temperature.

I lay in the luxury of an air-conditioned bedroom, thinking of the many different situations where I've had the wind in my face or behind my back. I recalled the edge of a tornado we'd weathered in a tent trailer on a high bluff above the Missouri River. Had we not left the trailer hooked to the car we might have been blown into the water. I recalled the May Day blizzard in a small town in South Dakota where we were snowbound for three days before they blasted the drifts so that we could reach the paved roads.

I remembered paddling a canoe, heavy with camping equipment, on our week-long trip into the wilderness when the wind was so severe in our faces we'd paddle three strokes forward and be pushed back two. Finally we had to pull into a cove to wait for the wind to change. I remembered the winds of the prairie that never quit, and how it was so dry that when I hung out clothes, the first ones I hung were dry by the time I finished hanging the last article. I remembered the cooling breezes on a hot summer night of my childhood before we had air conditioners. And I remembered sailing into the wind.

When I first learned about sailing I could not understand how a boat could move forward when the wind was not behind us. Anyone with common sense knew that a boat with a sail had to go in the direction of the wind! Right? Well, maybe it takes more than common sense, because I learned that you *can* make progress when the wind is against you. It involves a process called tacking.

With the boat angled into the wind, the sails are set at almost the same angle to the wind as the boat. The rudder is turned so as to maintain the boat's heading. In this way, the wind blows across the sail and the boat moves at an angle, but also in a forward direction. When you have gone as far as you can or want in that direction or "tack," you reverse your angle of attack into the wind, as well as your sails and your rudder, and you cut across the wind again, this time in the opposite direction, but still moving forward. In this way, you move on a zigzag course, but ever forward.

Yet whether you sail straight or by tacking, your goal, your destination, is the same. It's simply a matter of knowing how to handle the boat to reach it.

Sometimes it feels as if life is much like sailing into the wind. It seems that we must go out of our way, changing directions constantly, in order to get where we are going. We feel we are always in transition.

Transition, however, is not always bad. It can give us a different perspective of what's around us, and often we see something we never saw before because of a new point of view. Transition can also create new avenues and opportunities. As long as we set our goal and handle our lives properly, the transitions will move us forward to the goal. By working with the winds of transition, even though we go out of our way, we will continue on course.

I praise you, LORD, for being my guide.
Even in the darkest night, your teachings fill
my mind. I will always look to you, as you
stand beside me and protect me from fear.
With all my heart, I will celebrate,
and I can safely rest.

Psalms 16:7–9

Keep me on my goal, my Lord,
even when the winds blow strong in my face.
As I move through times of transition,
help me to see them as opportunities
and not as stone walls. Amen.

~ of waves and dunes

As I walked the flat sandy beach, I wondered "What is forever?" The ocean has been here a long time, constantly pounding waves on the shore. However, each day, as waves splash on the shore, they make new configurations of the sand dunes and over the years they completely reconfigure the shoreline.

I recalled the 13 years our family lived in North and South Dakota. That land was about as far away from the sea as you can get. Yet when the ranchers scooped out the earth to make a reservoir to water their cattle, they found shells among the piles of dirt. When I asked about this, having grown up in Florida, I was reminded that before any of our ancestors knew this land, before domesticated cattle roamed the range, there were no prairie grasses, only sea grasses – the land was covered with water.

As I continued to watch the waves beating on shore, I thought of the effects that hurricanes, tidal waves, and El Niño have had on many beaches, causing homes built too near the ocean to slide into the water. We sometimes create circumstances that bring about unwanted change when the alterations we make come into conflict with the normal, and not so normal, forces of nature.

But we cannot simply look back on the past as we knew it and say, "Oh to live in those good old days!" Creation itself was change – change from a deep, dark void to the world as we know it. When we were born, we went through the most drastic change we will probably ever experience in our lifetime, moving from a warm, comfortable but confined environment into one that allowed freedom to move arms and legs, and that contained bright light and unaccustomed sounds.

Change may seem good or change may seem not so good. But one thing is certain:

change is imminent. It *will* happen, and each year it happens at a faster rate.

So, what is forever? God is forever. And God is forever creating new people out of us, changing us, and allowing us to change the world around us.

> *Forget what happened long ago!*
> *Don't think about the past.*
> *I am creating something new.*
> *There it is! Do you see it?*
>
> Isaiah 43:18–19a

You are a God of change.
Without change, life would not be as we
know it today. However, I recognize your
steadfast love. You, yourself, will never
change. Thanks be to God. Amen.

~ of starfish and the nature of God

As a child, starfish were one of my favorite beach discoveries. On some days they were plentiful on the beach, and other times we seldom saw them. They always intrigued me, for when I approached one it would work its way into the sand with no apparent movement. Quickly, the sand just seemed to engulf the starfish.

I recall the first time that I saw a starfish without one of its legs. I voiced my concern to my parents. From their wisdom I was told that the leg would grow back. I thought that this was a great advantage. I had seen people who were missing a leg or an arm, and I wondered why God made starfish so that their legs regenerated but did not do the same with people. Such were my theological musings as a child.

I realize now that although God did not give us the ability to regenerate a limb, God *did* give us a far greater ability in the form of a mind.

And look at what that mind has done to develop replacements for limbs that are lost and to develop other means of protection. God has also given us the choice to live together in harmony and the tools of communication, understanding, and love to help that harmony to come about.

I continue to spend time reflecting about the nature of God and our relationship. Indeed, this is an essential part of our faith process, this need to question and to inquire. This is how we change and grow; this is how we open ourselves up to a deeper relationship with God.

And sometimes, as with the starfish, we cannot understand why God made things a certain way or why God doesn't intervene in certain situations. But behind it all, we recognize that we have a loving God. And we realize that God has given us the ability to adapt to a situation, whether it be loss of a limb or loss of a job. Although I don't believe God originally chose these painful situations for us, I do believe that God can use such transitions to help us become stronger persons and to deepen our relationships with other persons and with God.

You created me and put me together. Make me wise enough to learn what you have commanded.

Psalm 119:73

Life is often a mystery to us, O Lord.
Sometimes we puzzle over changes that
must come about in our lives.
But help us to remember to rely on you
to see us through those changes,
and give us the guidance to adapt.
Amen.

~ of turtle hatchlings and false gods

Several years ago we made our home on a coastal island in the Gulf of Mexico. The island had changed drastically from the first time we had visited it, back in the '60s. At that time we rented a small beach cottage with a large screened porch and no air conditioning. It was reminiscent of the cottages I had stayed in as a child. We even had trouble finding a restaurant on the island for an eat-out meal.

When we came to live in a small townhouse on the island we discovered condos and restaurants and shops and plush homes galore. And so I was surprised on the first night when we walked outside. There was no moon, but there were also no streetlights. It was almost as dark as I had experienced in our wilderness campsites or on moonless nights in the prairie states. When I quizzed the "natives" I learned the logical explanation. Because of the sea turtles, a ban was placed on streetlights and any beach property must have low wattage lighting at certain times of the year.

This island is a favorite nesting ground for the loggerhead sea turtles. These mammoth creatures (sometimes weighing up to 1,000 pounds) nest during the summer months. The female turtle comes ashore, digs a hole in the sand, and lays as many as 800 eggs. In due time the eggs hatch and the little turtles dig their way out of the sand. God has placed an instinct in these small hatchlings to move toward the light of the moon, shining on the sea. Unfortunately, our human desire to live daytime lives even in the dark of the night has caused us to brighten beaches with artificial light. And so, when there are bright lights on shore, the turtles move toward those false lights, finding themselves farther away from the water instead of swimming out to sea where they must go in order to survive.

As I recognize the perils that come to these hatchlings, I wonder about the false lights in my own life. What sort of "false gods" do I follow, thinking that they will give me a good life, while ignoring the true light? Might it be more money, a bigger house, a more prestigious career? Might it be children who enable me to "live" some childhood experiences I feel I missed? Might it even be a larger church, or a building, or a new project that would be a "monument" to me?

And is there someone else that I know who is in such a situation? Are my actions distracting them from the true light? How might I help that person to see the eternal light?

Your laws mean more to me than the finest gold. I follow all of your commands, but I hate anyone who leads me astray.

Psalms 119:127–128

Help me to keep the true light before me, my God. And put blinders on my eyes for all the other "false gods" in my life. Give me a push when I need to point the way to you for others. Amen.

~ of great white egrets and stewardship

As I headed for the beach, I stepped out on the boardwalk that spans the swampy backwater. Before me stood a lovely white sentinel, head erect and eyes alert. The long plumes, graceful in the breeze, were all that moved. I thanked God for such beauty!

Although I grew up near the Florida beaches, I don't recall the great white egret from my childhood. In fact, I have recently learned that there were very few of them at that time. We had almost wiped out this lovely bird to satisfy our own vain desires. During the early part of the century, women prided themselves in their large elaborate hats. The long white plumes that the egret grows during the mating season became very sought-after. These feathers were so valuable that merchants paid double the price of gold for each ounce of plumes. Hunters went into the swamps to find the nesting areas of the birds. There they indulged in mass slaughter, shooting the birds in their nests and scavenging the plumes, leaving their dead bodies on the floor of the swamp.

This lovely bird is not the only animal or plant that we have relentlessly brought to near-extinction. There are plants in the rain forests that are being burned every day. We are discovering that some of these plants have great medicinal powers. We may be destroying the cure for diseases that have recently gone rampant or the cure for diseases yet to emerge.

Such ruthless actions leave our environmental balance out of kilter. And with this behavior we have practiced poor stewardship. Consequently, in order to begin to reset the balance, we have had to change our lifestyles. Such changes may come hard.

At times, the need for a lifestyle transition comes about because of our own personal actions, but commonly such changes become necessary because of actions begun during past generations. Yet the people of those generations have been our models and teachers, and so we find it difficult to break the patterns they instilled in us. One such lifestyle is the independence that the automobile has given us. We are a culture of people who take pride in our independence. And when we are urged to conserve fuel and to carpool or use mass transportation, we rebel insisting that we need that automobile to maintain the independence that our forefathers died for.

And so we want to continue in the lifestyles we have come to find comfortable, and we find ourselves threatened by any change. Where does God's will come into the picture? Since God gave each individual a will of their own, if we are to act conscientiously we must discern ways to practice good stewardship. We face the decision, shall we fight to maintain life the way it has "always been"? Or can we search out ways to change our lifestyles, even when this will make us uncomfortable? What would God have us do?

> *The earth and everything on it*
> *belong to the LORD.*
> *The world and its people belong to [God].*
>
> Psalm 24:1

Oh God, help me to recognize and respect
change as a part of
your pattern and to appreciate
our part in your world. Amen.

~ of oysters and forgiveness

I have an oyster shell that sits on my desk – such an irregular shell, some would even call it ugly. In fact, unlike other shells, the oyster doesn't have a basic design. It seems to grow and take on a shape according to its surrounding circumstances and to where it attaches itself. In her book *Gift from the Sea*, Anne Morrow Lindbergh compares it to a house that has been pushed out and added to by a growing family. There is a hump here, an indention there, even an additional shell or barnacle attached to its back, giving the appearance of something added as an afterthought.

The exterior of the shell is rough and sharp, dangerous for those of us who enjoy barefoot beach walking. But when I turn it over, the interior of the shell is smooth and shines like a highly polished white tile floor. Such a contrast! And I appreciate the smooth interior of the shell even more after I have studied and felt the roughness of the exterior.

These mixed characteristics of the oyster remind me of the great contrast in various times in our lives, sometimes rough and dangerous and sometimes smooth and shining.

I had a friend once who had experienced very little disappointment in her life. I will always remember the time she hoped to attend a certain event and said, "If I really want something, it usually comes about!" Although my friend seldom faced disappointments, she was seldom filled with joy either. It seemed that she was always looking for the next big event to make her happy. Perhaps if she had had a little more disappointment in her life she would have cherished the good times more. Maybe if she had risked walking on the oyster shell and felt its sharp exterior, she would have appreciated the smooth luster of the interior.

The oyster shell that sits on my desk has my name printed in it and was the place card at a banquet in a church where I spoke. Fastened inside the open oyster shell is an imitation pearl. What a symbol! God has given the oyster an ability to make something of beauty out of an irritant. When a particle of sand makes its way into the shell of the oyster, the animal doesn't fret or give up, but it sets about immediately to make use of that irritant, coating it with a substance that covers the irritant, making it a new and lovely thing.

When we allow it, God does something like that for us, but we must surrender the irritant or problem or sin to God. Instead of digging at the irritant, we must turn it over to God. With God's forgiveness and grace, the irritant is coated with unconditional love and our life can become a thing of beauty. Our mistakes, wrapped in God's love, become like pearls.

I will lead the blind on roads they have never known; I will guide them on paths they have never traveled. Their road is dark and rough, but I will give light to keep them from stumbling. This is my solemn promise.

Isaiah 42:16

The rough places seem awfully sharp and fearful, God. Show me the smooth parts and help me recognize the beauty of them in contrast to the craggy parts of my life. I bring the irritants to you to be covered by your love. Thank you. Amen.

~ of fog and lighthouses

The sound echoed through the night, but I could hardly see beyond the tips of my fingers. Ordinarily, from where I sat, I could see large freighters passing. Even in the dark their lights usually outlined the horizon. But on this night a gray mist seemed to envelop the earth. For all I could tell, the world ended on the other side of my window glass.

There it was again, that haunting sound in the midst of the thick fog. Yes, no doubt about it, the warning sound of a ship's foghorn rang out loud and clear. The boat was out there, whether I could see it or not.

The fog made me think about my own vision. Do I know where I am going, or is fog obscuring my vision of God's direction for my life? Perhaps I use the fog as an excuse and ignore the foghorns that warn me of obstacles in my path. Do I turn a deaf ear and barrel down with determination to go my own route, only to collide with another ship?

Eventually, the horns were silent as I looked out into the night. I wondered where the ships were and if they had made a safe passing. In the silence, I suddenly saw a beam of light. It was the old lighthouse near the rocks at the entrance to the bay. Another warning, but more than a warning. This was also a guide. There was more direction here, for the ship knows that there are rocks near the lighthouse, and the light serves as a harbor point on which to take a bearing. Now the ship could be sure of the course, even in the sightless fog.

When we look for direction in knowing God's will, we need to talk it over with reliable models and mentors in our lives, as the ships communicate their locations by foghorns and radios. And we also need to pray and look to the Bible in order to find the true light that shines through the fog of our lives. If we take our bearings from that light, then we will make it safely along the rugged coast.

Once again Jesus spoke to the people. This time he said, "I am the light for the world! Follow me, and you won't be walking in the dark. You will have the light that gives life."

John 8:12

My God, give me the guidance to follow your will for my life. Help me to listen to your direction through prayer, study of your Word, and those models and mentors that you send my way. Amen.

~ of silt and tidal pools

Low tide is considered the best time for shelling. The higher tide has brought the shells up from the bottom of the ocean floor and dropped them on the beach. But on beaches that have a high population, the good shells are scooped up right away, leaving latecomers with empty shell bags. If you have done much shelling, however, you will know that there are a couple of other places to look for shells: the water's edge and tidal pools.

As I walked along the edge of the surf I spotted a small, bright orange shell – one of my favorites. Quickly, trying to beat the wave, I scooped up a handful of shells. Opening my hand, I found no orange shell, only small broken pieces of shells. I spent the next five minutes, looking for my little shell. The waves continued to wash over the shore, stirring up a storm of shell pieces, silt, and foam, preventing any sighting of my tiny shell. I reached down into the silt and came up time and again with a handful of broken pieces.

Finally I realized that the waves were no longer washing over the place where I was looking. The tide had receded enough to leave a lovely little tidal pool before me. As I watched, the waters began to calm and slowly the silt sank to the bottom. Within a few minutes, I had clear water and could see everything on the bottom of the small hollow in the beach. There was my small orange horse conch, and dozens of other small shells scattered below the surface. I no longer had to fight the waves. I no longer came up with handfuls of unwanted shell particles. I settled down on the edge of the pool to marvel over the clarity of choices before me.

I thought about how much our lives are like the surf and the tidal pools. We set our sights on a goal and struggle against the surf to acquire it. But time and again we come up empty-handed. Sometimes we need transitional periods or times in limbo so that the "silt" can settle out and we can see clearly.

Please make me wise and teach me the difference between right and wrong.

1 Kings 3:9a

*God, you are my calming force.
With you I can wait out the surf.
Give me patience to stop my thrashing
about and to look into
the clear tidal pools of my life. Amen.*

Driftwood
Maturity and Experience

As a child I did not appreciate driftwood. Perhaps I did not have the experience to understand the beauty of maturity, or perhaps it was simply my inability to think as abstractly as I can as an adult. I now have several pieces of driftwood that we have moved from place to place. They are as valuable to us as an expensive lamp or a quality painting. In fact, some pictures that we've valued in the past now lean against the wall in our attic, but the driftwood remains on the shelf or beside the door. There is a beauty of form and shape in the driftwood that I see. But there is more than that. There is a heritage, reminding me that gray is beautiful and weathered lines give witness to experience.

~ of birds in formation

My first introduction to the ibis was a rather messy one. We were not living near the sea at the time, and we were spending a few days with friends on their houseboat. This particular day we had docked at a national park, and our friends suggested that we visit an area where the ibis come to roost every evening. As we watched, a flock flew in for a landing. I was thrilled that they seemed to be coming right over where we stood. I anticipated getting a close-up view of the lovely white bird, with its curved orange bill. I got a closer view than I desired. One bird chose to leave his mark on my head! Needless to say, I headed for the showers.

This experience clouded my opinion of the ibis for some time until I recognized some of the wisdom of the bird. The ibis, like geese, fly in a V-formation when flying distances. By experience these birds have learned that working in community can get you where you are going more quickly and easily. Studies have determined that birds that fly in formation have at least 71 percent greater flying range than if each bird flew on its own. As each bird flaps its wings, it creates an uplift for the bird that is immediately following. When a bird falls out of formation, it feels the drag and resistance of trying to fly alone. By quickly getting back into formation, the bird takes advantage of that lifting power of cooperative action.

When we share a common goal as a community, as a family, as a church, we accomplish that goal more quickly and easily when we work together. Yet, in our culture, we have stressed independence for so many years that we have forgotten the importance of *inter*dependence. We may create a beautifully worded mission statement, but then we assign one part of that goal to one group and another part of the goal to different group. We turn the groups loose and say, "Go and do your thing! Report back when you're through." Then we are surprised, or perhaps even angry, when the different groups duplicate their agendas. We judiciously guard our own little budget or property, never offering help to other groups. We have lost the maturity of the ibis!

God created us in community. Truly, none of us is an island unto our self.

God is the one who makes us patient and cheerful. I pray that [God] will help you live at peace with each other, as you follow Christ.

Romans 15:5

God, grant me the wisdom
and maturity of the ibis.
Where there is division,
help me to bring unity. Amen.

~ of camouflaged birds and conformity

Some coastal regions have a strange phenomenon, a very marshy area just behind a string
of barrier islands. Sidney Lanier brought my
attention to these areas in his poem *The Marshes
of Glynn*. Lanier speaks of the marsh hen that
builds her nest in the grasses. But there is another bird that makes the marshes its home.
We could learn from this bird too.

The American bittern is a medium-size bird
with cream coloring and streaks of brown. The
bird usually stands erect among the grasses,
lifting its head. This causes the brown streaks
on its body to blend in with the tall grasses. In
fact, even when you know the bird is there
among the grasses before you, it is almost impossible to see. Not only does the bird's coloring blend in with its surroundings, but this
bittern has learned to imitate the movement
of its surroundings. As the wind blows and

moves the grasses, the bird sways, further camouflaging its body.

We could learn from the American bittern. There are times when we need to blend with those around us in order to be effective, and there are times when we must stand out and speak up.

When I was in college, I had a very wise and mature anthropology professor. She passed on a bit of her wisdom to our class. For years she had battled for acceptance by her colleagues, even though she had her PhD in anthropology. Dr. Ina C. Brown told us that she had learned that one must sometimes conform in minor things in order to have some influence in more important things. One of her ways of conforming was to wear earrings. (Large earrings were popular at that time.) Dr. Brown did not like earrings, but she had noticed that when she wore them people were more likely to listen to what she had to say. I can still see her blue earrings and appreciate the maturity of her thinking.

Sometimes we blatantly parade our convictions in front of the world, only to have the world shoot us down. At those times we would be much more effective if we followed Jesus' example. He went about his ministry in a quiet way instead of forcing it on people. He got to know the people first, and he met their needs. Then he was able to tell them about God. When the people saw his example, they were ready to listen to his words. Paul said, "When you are with unbelievers, always make good use of the time. Be pleasant and hold their interest when you speak the message. Choose your words carefully and be ready to give answers to anyone who asks questions" (Colossians 4:5–6).

Everything on earth has its own time. There is a time for...listening and speaking.

Ecclesiastes 3:1, 2a, 7

*Patience is what I need, my God,
and wisdom to know when to conform
or to keep silent and when to speak out
for what I believe.
Help me to learn from others. Amen.*

~ of scallops and simplicity

I ran my hand through the pile of calico scallop shells, looking for those with bright pink coloring. When I discovered that some of the shells were much brighter than others, common sense told me that those with dull color had been washed ashore earlier and had spent more time bleaching in the sun. But it was puzzling that some of the shells were not pink or purple at all, but rather a dark gray, almost black. I even found a shell that had both parts intact with one of the halves a colorful pink and the other quite dark gray. Curious about this, I went to my shell book. I learned that a calico scallop will lose its bright color and turn dark when buried in muck so that no oxygen is present.

This made me wonder about myself and my life. What is the "muck" of my life? Perhaps it is the everydayness of life. Perhaps I am digging into the muck when I allow insignificant things to take priority over the experiences I need to emphasize. Perhaps the "muck" is an addiction, or a tendency to procrastinate.

Time is a gift from God. We are each given 24 hours every day, no more and no less, and we are stewards of that time. How we use it makes a difference in whether we are able to accomplish our goals. To be stewards of our time we must prioritize, center ourselves, and keep foremost in our minds the important use of our God-given time.

Simplifying our lives also helps to remove the muck. When we focus on the direction that we believe God to be calling us and make that a measuring rod for our decisions, then our lives become simplified, even when they are full. We need to answer the simple question, "Does this help or hinder my following God's call?" The answer to that question can remove the muck from our lives.

What happens to me when I bury myself in the muck of everyday life and don't come into contact with God? Just as the calico scallop needs oxygen to retain its bright pink or purple color, I need union with God to have the oxygen for my soul. That building of relationship with God happens in different ways for different people. Some people find short, daily periods of prayer and meditation most helpful, while others of us must find less frequent but larger blocks of time to set aside for study and reflection, as well as for prayer. Whatever the method, prayer remains one of the best ways to loosen the muck and wash it away.

Right away, Jesus made his disciples get into the boat and start back across to Bethsaida. But he stayed until he had sent the crowds away. Then he told them goodbye and went up on the side of a mountain to pray.

Mark 6:45–46

*Draw me close to you, O God,
and give me the courage to loosen
the muck from my life. Amen.*

~ of safety rails and God's grace

It amazes me how the natural surroundings of our childhood often affect our comfort level. My mother grew up on the plains of New Mexico and north Texas. When she encountered the timbered mountains of the east, she was not very happy. She said she felt closed-in because she couldn't see around her. But when she could look out across the ocean, whether at sea level or on an overlook, she experienced release and freedom.

On the other hand, I grew up in the midst of trees. The nooks and crannies of a forested area, along with the heavy canopy overhead, give me a sense of protection. The wide open spaces can make me feel vulnerable, with no place to hide.

With maturity and many moves to different areas, however, my mother and I both learned to live in a variety of settings. As we moved about we said, like Paul, "I've learned to live in whatever state I am."

I have an e-mail friend who is short in stature. When telling about an adventure with cliffs she said, "I'm under five feet and afraid of high places." But she added, "There are some high places that are great, as long as there are safety rails." I've heard of God referred to as a safety net, why not safety rails?

Safety rails give us opportunity to go where we wouldn't dare to go otherwise. There are many places that God leads us and many plans for ministry that we'd never feel comfortable about without knowing that God is there with us.

Safety rails are also tall enough to offer protection, yet short enough to allow us a sense of freedom. God's grace is something like that, offering us protection and unconditional love, yet giving us freedom to choose for ourselves and forgiveness when we fail.

You give me strength and guide me right. You make my feet run as fast as those deer, and you help me stand on the mountains.

Psalm 18:32–33

Oh, that I may find you in the high places,
and the low places as well.
Guide my feet and give me safety rails,
so that I may see your splendor
yet exercise independence. Amen.

~ of the vast ocean

As I look out over the sea it appears to be un-ending. I can see nothing on the other side. No wonder people used to believe that you would sail off the end of the earth if you got out of sight of land. The sea was unstable and un-known, the black depths a true mystery. Even today, with such a vast expanse of ocean, we still tend to place our confidence in the solid earth, which we can feel firm beneath our feet. There's a vastness we have only begun to ex-plore.

If we had to judge based only on our own experience, it would be hard to believe that three-fourths of the earth's surface is covered with water – 97.4 percent of it salt water. And it's so much more than just a thin covering. Beneath the surface are mountains and valleys, vast unexplored worlds covered with water. When we try to grasp just how much water there is in the oceans, our mind boggles.

I'm reminded of the hymn we sang when I was a child, a hymn we still sing today.

> There's a wideness in God's mercy, Like the wideness of the sea;
> There's a kindness in His justice, Which is more than liberty.[1]

Yet, as vast as the ocean is before me, with all its unplumbed depths, God's love is even greater. The amount of water in the ocean is only a drop when compared to the vastness of God's love. And that love is offered to me at no price. I don't have to work for it, to buy it, or even to make a promise. It's there for the taking. This is God's grace.

I never understood the term "grace" as I was growing up, until someone gave me a definition that helped me. Grace is a "love you anyway" type love. It's a love that is limitless, even more vast than the waters of the sea.

But you, the LORD God, are kind and
merciful. You don't easily get angry,
and your love can always be trusted.

Psalm 86:15

Your love is so great, my God,
that I can't comprehend it.
I will try not to take it for granted,
and I will try to share with others
the vastness of your love. Amen.

[1] by Frederick W. Faber, p.18 in *The Cokesbury Worship Hymnal*,
Abingdon, 1966.

~ of trees and interdependence

Trees along the shore tell a story of land and sea. The native trees on particular shores have evolved according to the environmental circumstances. Where there are high winds, palms grow in quantity. These trees offer little wind resistance, with their long, slender trunks. The branches bend with the wind, and the fronds allow the wind to move through freely.

In northern climes where there is snow and ice, evergreens border the shore. These trees are able to endure the cold temperatures. Their shape and the glossy needles allow them to shed the snow.

The first time I visited the South Carolina and Georgia coast, I was surprised to see the live oak trees. In fact, these trees did not even look like the huge, sprawling live oaks I'd known in central Florida. The trees reminded me of the shaped trees of Japan, with their bent and sweeping branches, leaning away from shore. When I viewed the trees from the beach their tops were low and curved, as if they were a part of the sand dunes, just a different color. I learned that the live oaks along the coast had adapted to their environment. Because of strong winds from the sea, the trees grew low to the ground. The shape allowed the winds to blow over the sand dunes and on across the tops of the trees, causing little damage.

Nature is the best example God gives us of maturity and experience. Some people may call it survival of the fittest, but that concept is too independent for my definition of maturity. I like to think of it as interdependence, learned from experience. A mature person recognizes that neither independence nor total dependence is good, but that we must practice interdependence. God set up the world that way.

*Show me your ways, O LORD, teach me your
paths; guide me in your truth and teach me,
for you are God my Savior,
and my hope is in you all day long.*

Psalm 25:4–5 (New International Version)

*My God, only you can give me true maturity.
Use your world to teach me what
maturity is. Help me to remember
that there is always some opportunity for
growth in a mature person. Amen.*

Beachcombers
People in Our Lives

Such a variety of folks God made. I must marvel at such diversity. Yet each person is a special creation of God and is loved as much by God as any other person. And there is so much to learn and to be gained from these folk. I must stay alert to every person's contribution to my life.

~ of all sorts of folk

It was early morning when I awoke, and there was a slight pink tinge to the sky. I could hear the gentle rumbling of the cruise ship. We had lifted anchor in the night and headed out to sea. I dressed quickly and made my way to the aft deck, hoping to see the sunrise. I wasn't disappointed.

A huge ball of orange began to rise from the sea and spread God's glory in all directions, embracing the world. Above me the clouds began to take shape. Some seemed to be in the image of animals; some might have been mountains in the sky; some simply billows of pink cotton candy. Two other people were sitting on deck with me. Everyone else aboard seemed to be sleeping. Such a large ship of people, all of us headed in the same direction, but with such varied interests.

I began to reflect on friends in the Bible, some with common backgrounds and varied interests, and some with varied backgrounds and common interests.

* Jacob and Esau were from the same biological family, yet their varied interests caused them to come to a deep division.
* Ruth and Naomi, from completely different cultures, found a common bond in their love for each other and in their understanding of God.
* Mary and Elizabeth were separated by years, or we might say by a generation gap, but their common calling bound them together.
* There was never a more varied group of 12 friends than the disciples that Jesus chose. But Jesus knew each one of them and knew what they could contribute to his mission.
* Paul and Barnabas had a common mission, yet there were specific things that they could not agree on, and so they parted ways, each using his individual gifts to carry out God's mission.

God made us each different. Without that difference, we could not accomplish God's plan. It's important for us each to learn to recognize our individual specialties and to set about developing those talents and using them for God.

The body of Christ has many different parts, just as any body does. Some of us are Jews, and others are Gentiles. Some of us are slaves, and others are free. But God's Spirit baptized each of us and made us part of the body of Christ. Now we each drink from that same Spirit.

1 Corinthians 12:12–13

Thank you, God, for making me special in my own way. Help me to recognize the specialness of others. Amen.

~ of shell collectors
and caretakers

One of the favorite jokes that gets told along the coast of Florida is that the best place to find shells is on the Florida-Georgia border. About the time folks cross the state line on their way home, the shells, which were alive when they picked them up off the beach, have died and begun to smell so bad that they discard them.

Because so many live shells were taken in the past 40 years and the shell population has decreased drastically, we now have laws against taking live shells. We must learn to live in harmony with the world that God has given us.

In Genesis we read that God gave humans dominion over the earth. That does not mean that God gave the earth to us to do with as we please. Rather we are to rule over it justly, to take into consideration the way that God created the earth and see that it is maintained in that balance. It has taken years of study to understand the balance in nature. Without scientists investigating such matters, we would be in an even worse situation than we are today. I thank God for those people who impact my life by their studies. I thank God for persons who continually watch and monitor our stewardship of the earth, even when they don't recognize their role as stewards.

There was a time when I also took a few live shells. But now I have a better understanding of my responsibility to the whole earth. My shells may not be as large, but every time I find a live shell I recognize my part in caring for the world by throwing it back into the sea.

Teach me to follow you, and I will obey your truth. Always keep me faithful.

Psalm 86:11

It is so easy, Lord, to forget about the people and the parts of the earth that have no immediate bearing on my life each day. Help me to be aware of and respect every part of your world. Take away the selfish, arrogant attitude of manipulation that I may have when I want to do as I please with your earth. Amen.

~ of folks and serving

The beach is a great place for solitude, and this particular morning I needed solitude in order to make a decision. But as I stepped out on the beach, it appeared that everyone within driving distance had also come to the beach for solitude! I felt thwarted, and so I tried to block out an awareness of other persons as I walked along the shore.

I took a leisurely path, sometimes on the edge of the surf and sometimes in the grasses. Occasionally I simply stopped and looked at the grand expanse of the sea. Finally I realized that I was not being very successful in my search for solitude, because a mother and her young child continued to draw my attention. The woman had a worried expression on her face. It was as if God was prodding me to speak to them. I picked up a shell and approached the boy.

I showed the child my shell and asked if he knew the name of it. I explained that it is called a slipper shell because it is shaped something like a slipper. I suggested that he place his finger in the shell and pretend to "walk" it on the sand. With a smile, the boy experimented with the slipper shell as his mother and I began to talk. I learned that she was a single mom with very little time for her son but a real concern for his emotional and spiritual development. We walked along the beach for about an hour, talking in the freshness of the morning. As we parted there was a smile on her face, and she thanked me for taking the time to talk with them. I had missed my time of solitude, but as I began my day I realized that my own problem and decision had worked itself out, or perhaps I should say God had worked on the problem while I showed concern for my new friends.

I never saw the woman and child again, but I learned one valuable lesson from them. I learned to pay attention when God gives us an opportunity for service, even when the service is a listening ear.

After Jesus heard about John, he crossed Lake Galilee to go to some place where he could be alone. But the crowds found out and followed him on foot from the towns. When Jesus got out of the boat, he saw the large crowd. He felt sorry for them and healed everyone who was sick.

Matthew 14:13–14

Help me to remain aware of those around me, my God. Help me to remember that I do not always need to solve my problems in solitude. When I follow your calling, even when it takes me from solitude, then I can see more clearly myself. Amen.

~ of folks sung to
and folks singing

Every section of the country has some sort of tree that appears to be weeping. This is true of the shore along large bodies of water and also along small, inland seas. The Japanese, with their appreciation for ponds and sea, have included these weeping trees in much of their art. As a child, my mother's dishes were blue and white, with a Japanese design of willows, bridges, and water.

Many a day I looked at the design on the dishes, recalling the story that my mother told to go along with the scene. I have no idea how much of the story was the actual legend and how much she embellished. But her version of the story was of a young man and woman who fell in love. The parents did not want them to marry and would disown them if they did. The couple ran away in the boat that was sailing to an island, and the three men who were walking across a bridge with a lantern were looking for the young woman to take her back home. There was a willow tree on the shore and two lovebirds over the tree. There was no ending to the story, and I often wondered if the couple got away or not. Then I reasoned, even if they did get away, how sad it would be not to have your parents a part of your life too.

As an adult, the willow tree and that story remind me of the passage in Psalm 132, when the psalmist recalls their time in Babylon, and how they were challenged to sing of Zion. They felt they could not sing. All they could do was hang their harps on the willow tree and sit down and cry. There are times when folks need to sing, and there are certainly times when folks need to be allowed to cry and to be sung to themselves.

Beside the rivers of Babylon we thought about Jerusalem, and we sat down and cried. We hung our small harps on the willow trees.

Psalm 137:1–2

God of the willows and God of the harps,
there are times when the tears flow
and I cannot sing. At these times
I must rely on you to send someone to sing
to me. I may even need to speak up myself
and ask someone else to sing
while my harp hangs from the branch.
I also ask that you give me insight
to know when to ask someone
to join me in singing and when to
take the harp off the willow tree
and sing to someone else myself. Amen.

~ of people on the run

One of the most enjoyable gifts found along the sea is the joy of watching the energetic sandpipers as they scurry along the beach. Their thin legs sometimes move so fast that I can only see a blur of movement. I have a delightful nature video that puts music from *The Flight of the Bumble Bee* to their running feet, and indeed that is an appropriate combination.

As entertaining as these little birds are, however, when I watch them they remind me of rushed periods in my life. Like the birds, sometimes I start out hurrying in one direction, only to be distracted and turn my course of direction to trivial matters. At times I seem to rush off by myself, ignoring the crowd. At other times I scurry after nothing, right along with everyone else, never stopping to investigate what is around me. We are forever people on the run.

Be Still, My Soul is a hymn we used to sing more often than we do now. The second verse reminds us that God will guide our future as God has guided people in ages past. Evidently this tendency to scurry off in all directions has been a problem across the generations. Written in 1752, the hymn is based on words the psalmist wrote thousands of years ago.

I may smile at the antics of the sandpipers, but I can also learn from them that God is my center and the one to whom I must look for direction.

Be still my soul, they God doth undertake. To guide the future as He has the past. They hope, they confidence let nothing shake, all now mysterious shall be bright at last. Be still my soul, the waves and winds still know His voice who ruled them while He dwelt below.

Our God says, "Calm down,
and learn that I am God!"

Psalm 46:10a

It seems I always have a "have to" list,
Lord. Sometimes it gets so full that
I don't know in which direction to go first.
Help me to keep my eyes upon you
and to allow you to be God. Amen.

Treasures Among the Grasses
Unexpected and Hidden Moments

Too often we go through life as if we had blinders on. Now blinders may be an understandable necessity for horses, because the owner has only one purpose in mind for the horse – to accomplish a specific task. But when we place blinders on ourselves we miss many a hidden moment or unexpected treasure.

~ of marshes and mud

The 19th-century poet laureate Sidney Lanier had great appreciation for marshes, particularly the marshes in Glenn County, on the Georgia coast. All my life I had heard of the Marshes of Glenn, but seeing them for the first time was a captivating experience.

My idea of a marsh had been something like a swamp or a bog. I expected them to be muddy looking. But instead, these famed marshes on the southeast coast of North America held a calm beauty. In fact, they looked clean and perfect as I viewed them from a distance. Nothing seemed out of place. They reminded me of the wheat fields I'd known when we lived in the Dakotas.

There were saltwater canals running through the marsh, like veins in an aging hand. We put our canoe into the water at the edge of the marsh and set out to explore. We discovered a whole ecosystem that was not obvious from a distance. Fiddler crabs scurried among the grasses, with their large pincher "fiddling" before them. They shoveled mud into their mouths, sieving out the food, and discarded the rest in small balls of earth. Mussels and oysters emerged from the mud, and periwinkle snails gleaned microorganisms from the leaf surfaces of the grass. Later, we learned that what we could see was only the tip of an eco-system iceberg. As quickly as a leaf of grass died, it was shredded and consumed by the multitude of microscopic animals to begin the cycle over again.

How often we cast a passing glance at God's world, seeing only the surface. Or we go about observing only those things that directly impact ourselves, not even aware of what affects other people. We must leave our known and comfortable places and search the unknown to appreciate the intricacies of the world.

I will praise you, LORD,
with all my heart and tell about
the wonders you have worked.

Psalm 9:1

Creator God, your world is so great.
It takes more than a league of scientists
to comprehend just what is happening
in the natural world,
and no one can really understand it.
I do praise you for allowing me
to be a part of this wonder. Amen.

~ of egg cases and God's care

The sun broke through as I stepped out on the beach. Yesterday's storm had hit at the same time as a high tide, and the water had reached well into the grassy dunes. I decided to walk among those grasses instead of along the water's edge. Many treasures hide among grasses after such a high tide.

That morning I found something that looked like brown artificial Hawaiian lei, similar to those I remembered from my childhood. As a child I thought it to be a form of seaweed and collected several of the strands, pretending to be a hula dancer. My ignorance as a child and my lack of inquisitiveness had kept me from discovering one of God's tiny surprises. The lightning whelk's egg case may have as many as 25 individual pockets, and each pocket may contain 20 to 100 tiny whelks. The number of miniature whelks will depend on whether the small animals have begun eating each other.

This cannibalistic characteristic is a part of the natural mechanism that God created to provide food during the whelk's incubation period.

This particular egg case was dry and stiff, and so I knew that the shells inside would not be alive. I opened a pocket, and tiny whelks spilled into my palm. I marveled over the intricate shells, each a true miniature of the parent shell. I wondered how anything so small could have such perfect detail! If God cares enough to make this tiny shell, then God must care about me.

It puzzles me that so many people dwell on the sinfulness of our nature instead of the positive, loving care of God. Do those folks need to live in the dark in order to appreciate the light? I would think that once they recognized God's love they would be ready to put the dark days behind them and spend their time simply basking in God's love and sharing it with others. Then living the Christian life becomes a joy, not because we must resist temptation, but because we want to follow the positive example that Christ set.

All we need to do is look around us to see God's love exhibited in the small surprises in the grasses; in the glory of color spangled across the sky at sunset; in the music of the waves; and in the people in our lives.

Five sparrows are sold for just two pennies, but God doesn't forget one of them. Even the hairs on your head are counted. So don't be afraid! You are worth much more than many sparrows.

Luke 12:6–7

Thank you, God, for the joys of your world,
those hidden and those obvious.
I will look to your love instead of
dwelling on my sinfulness. Amen.

~ of jellyfish and spinelessness

The sea holds many extremes. Perhaps the most dramatic is the spinelessness of a jellyfish and the strength and determination of a tarpon.

There are many types of jellyfish, and most of them are difficult to see unless you look at them from the right angle. (They will, however, let you know of their presence when you bump into them. Their stinging cells can give your skin a temporary burning sensation.)

The moon jellyfish, for example, is fairly common and is a very graceful swimmer. It looks a lot like a plastic bag or partially de-flated balloon. Then there's the comb jellyfish – very small (two to five inches) and not a true jellyfish. It does not sting. It is almost totally transparent in the daytime. (It *is*, however, luminous and glows at night. The eight "comb rows" of very fine hairs beat rhythmically when the animal swims, creating a fascinating play of iridescent light often enjoyed by night fishermen.)

On the other extreme is the tarpon. Its silver body is very visible, and its determination to be free excites any who take fishing seriously. The tarpon will fight so violently it can raise its large body high above the water, pulling a boat with its force. The only way to safely land a tarpon is to set the hook and then tire it out first with play in the line.

Is my Christian life like a jellyfish, transparent and spineless? Do I bend my morals to fit the surroundings and other people's opinions? Or am I like a tarpon, proud to be who I am and firm in my actions?

*But if you don't want to worship the LORD,
then choose right now!...My family and I are
going to worship and obey the LORD!*

Joshua 24:15a, c

*My God, in your wisdom you created the
jellyfish without a spine. But you have not
only given me a spine but also an ability to
choose. Help me overcome my spinelessness.
Amen.*

~ of crabs and comprehension

Most seashore visits happen in the daytime. We usually associate the beach with fun in the sun. But there are some exciting things to discover on night excursions, especially among the tall grasses alongshore.

I grew up with fiddler crabs. From my experience, I expected all crabs to be plain brown in color and certainly not very pretty creatures. Then I discovered the colorful calico crab, which has spots similar to that of a tiger. This crab spends most of its time in the water, however fragments of its shell may be found along the beaches. But my big surprise in crab sightings was the one that comes out at night from among the grasses, the ghost crab.

The mature ghost crab is rather yellow in coloring, with large white pinchers. If you do catch this crab scuttling about in the early evening, its color is intensified by the sunlight and shadows. However, the crab gets its name from the juvenile of the species. This young crab truly has a ghostlike appearance; it is white, and speckled with gray. The color blends so well with the sand that it is impossible to see unless a flashlight is shone on it, or it moves in the moonlight. Although it is unobtrusive, the juvenile ghost crab goes about its work of digging burrows and searching for food. Periodically, this land-based crab scurries to the water's edge to wet its gills in order to stay alive.

As I watched the little sand-colored crab, I wondered what of importance I sometimes overlook simply because I'm looking for something much more flashy? Do I ignore the quiet voice as I listen for the pounding drums? Do I recognize the gift of love and of excitement that young children bring into my life? Do I look for the positive in a person, even when someone has told me something negative about them? What am I missing when I don't take time to look among the grasses of life?

The religious leaders of Jesus' day were looking for someone to fill the role of the Messiah, but they were looking for a glitzy leader. Consequently they overlooked the Messiah. They could not believe that someone so powerful could come in such a plain wrapper as the body of a carpenter.

When Jesus and his disciples were near the
town of Caesarea Philippi, he asked them,
"What do people say about the Son of Man?"
The disciples answered,
"Some people say you are
John the Baptist or maybe Elijah
or Jeremiah or some other prophet."
Then Jesus asked them,
"But who do you say I am?"
Simon Peter spoke up, "You are the
Messiah, the Son of the living God."

Matthew 16:13–16

Help me, O God, to recognize the
obscure but important messengers
that you send. Amen.

~ of nests among the grasses

At this particular beach, the grassy area stretches back quite a distance from the shore. There are many surprises if you take the time to walk here. The yellow face of the beach sunflower may poke its head up from the groundcover vine. Or you might find various insects buzzing among the lavender and purple blooms of the railroad vine, also known as the beach morning glory. The yellow blooms of the prickly pear cactus will greet you in its season. There are sea oats and other grasses along the dunes.

But be careful as you walk. You may come upon the home of a burrowing owl. This little critter, with surprisingly long legs, will proudly stand erect on the mound beside its nest-home. It tolerates humans at a fairly close range, but when agitated it will bob and bow. As the burrowing owl's sandy habitat is taken over by large homes and manicured lawns, its place in the ecological balance is endangered.

Why do we thwart the natural balance that God created? The burrowing owl may establish its home in the sandy back-dunes of the beach, but God gave it wings to fly elsewhere when impeding storms threaten. When the waters recede, those dunes may be gone, but it adjusts by digging a new burrow in a new location. When we build close to the shore in the sea storm's path, not only do we destroy the natural surroundings, but we insist that our "sacred" land be preserved, even against the earth's natural evolutionary processes. We spend untold monies rebuilding houses and refurbishing beaches that have previously survived centuries of shifting up and down the coastline. We seem to think we can control the earth, when actually God put us here as stewards of the earth rather than conquerors.

*Birds build their nests nearby
and sing in the trees.*

Psalm 104:12

*I praise you, God, for the intricate manner in
which you created the world. I will try to
become a better steward of that which you
have put into my care. Amen.*

~ of nesting birds
and night flowers

It was our first year of life on the island, and we were still learning about its seasons. When we left our previous home, everyone asked us how we could live at a place that had no seasons. During that first year on the island we discovered even more seasons than in our former home; they were just more subtle and you had to tune your eye to an awareness. There were the seasons of specific flowering plants; the seasons of certain birds; seasons when butterflies were more profuse; seasons when trees put on new growth.

During that first year I recall a sudden excitement that spread across the island. The yellow-crowned night herons were nesting! This was a MUST on everyone's list, but especially for newcomers to the island. We made our way to the wildlife refuge for the nature show. The refuge had several lakes and canals made up of a mixture of salt and fresh water, and along one of those canals we spent some time observing the current season's phenomenon. Above the canal, branches hung over the water and a colony of yellow-crowned night herons had built their nests. Normally, these birds build nests 15 to 50 feet above the ground as a protection from predators. However, less than 20 feet away from us, at eye level, these placid birds incubated their eggs. And below them lounged several alligators. The birds had learned that nesting above the favorite sunning sites of alligators offered good protection. Their normal predators, such as the raccoon and possum, kept their distance or they became dinner for the alligators themselves.

A little later that same year we discovered the season of the night blooming cereus. I had spent several months on the island and often wondered why people cultivated the thick, gangly twining plant that crawled up the trees and looped from the branches. I really considered it an eyesore. It looked much like a green snake with ridges up its sides, draping itself among the branches and crawling over everything in sight. And then the season of the night blooming cereus came, and the evening was filled with a scent like a fine French perfume. The dazzling whiteness of this dinner-plate sized flower stood out brightly, illuminating the night like so many moons amid the darkness. Beyond the apparent ugliness was a divine purpose, to bloom and glorify God with beauty and fragrance.

Yes, there are seasons everywhere. Where seasons are subtle, we must be more alert to change. And perhaps in watching for these subtle changes, we learn to develop an awareness of God that we would miss otherwise.

Everything on earth has its own time and its own season.

Ecclesiastes 3:1

Help me to appreciate the uniqueness of your world, God. From the serene perfection of the heron to the tangled mass of the night blooming cereus, give me joy in every season of your earth. Amen.

Shells for the Taking
Recognizing the Obvious

Do you recall the saying, "If it had been a snake, it would have bitten you"? This was one of my mother's favorite sayings when I couldn't find something that she'd sent me to find. Perhaps our inability to see things that are right before our eyes is actually a lack of interest. Or perhaps God has given some people an ability to be more observant. But we often miss God right before our eyes if we don't continue to look for the evidence.

~ of clams and choices

There are two primary classifications of shells, the bivalves and the univalves. Most univalve shells are spiral in shape, and the live animals are marine snails. The bivalve shells have two sections that are hinged like a door. The animal that lives in the bivalve uses muscles that are attached to the inside to open the shell and draw in food or to extend a siphon-tube for feeding.

I learned that this label for shells comes from an old English use of the word valve, which applied to a panel of a folding door. Immediately I thought of the verse from the Bible that inspired the famous painting by William Holman Hunt, "The Light of the World." In this painting, Christ is standing at a door with a lantern in his hand, knocking to be allowed to enter. The picture speaks of choice, a choice that is ours to make, a choice of opening our hearts to Jesus or holding them shut from within.

If you have ever tried to pry open a clam or an oyster without cooking it first, you know that it is almost impossible to do so. There are no handles or latches that can be lifted from the outside, just as Hunt painted the door in his picture with no exterior handle. The decision to open must come from within. The clam must choose to open the bivalves. Christ will not force us to open our hearts. Christ's love is freely given, but unless we choose to open our hearts and our lives to that love, then we can never receive it; we can never be fed that sustenance which gives us true life.

I have a friend who wears a pendant that is a replica of a door. She prefers to wear this instead of a cross. In recent years we have allowed the cross to become just another piece of jewelry. Indeed, there are persons today wearing crosses who model anything but a Christian lifestyle. My friend has also found that when she wears the door pendant people will ask her about it, and this gives her opportunity to share some thoughts with the inquirer.

I've looked for such a pendant but have not found one yet. Perhaps a closed bivalve shell might serve the same purpose.

Listen! I am standing and knocking at your door. If you hear my voice and open the door, I will come in and we will eat together.

Revelation 3:20

*My God, there are times when my
hinges become rusty and my door
handle is covered with vines.
I need to lubricate the hinges with some
elbow grease and release the latch with a
smile. Come into my heart, Lord Jesus.
Amen.*

~ of boat shells and the church

I stopped to watch a child play in a tidal pool. As we sat on the sand together he pushed a small shell across the top of the water, shouting gleefully, "See, it's a boat!" The slipper shell does look like a boat, with a little seat on one end.

I did a little research in the concordance and realized that the word boat is not used in the Old Testament at all, except in the Noah story where the translations usually call the vessel an ark. In the New Testament, the word is only used in the gospels and in the record of Paul's shipwreck. Going out to sea was a fearsome experience in biblical times. Jonah thought that he could escape God's demands by running away to sea. Some people believed that God did not care for them at sea because so much happened to seafaring people that was beyond explanation. We tend to either blame God or completely ignore God in times of disaster.

Christ, however, frequently made use of the boat, and these times are recorded in the gospels. He must have enjoyed the sea because he took every opportunity to be near it. In early Christendom the boat became a symbol of the church, a safe place for people to sail across the rough seas of life. In an early document there were orders to build churches oblong, toward the east, like a ship. Gothic architecture looks like a ship turned upside down. There is a church on Ft. Myers Beach, Florida, designed in a nautical theme. The lights are modified ship's wheels, the pulpit looks like the bow of a boat, the communion table is designed like the hatch of the deck, and the cross is in the style of a mast. The congregation is surrounded by reminders of the importance of the church in their Christian life.

We call the section of the church building where the congregation sits the "nave." This stems from the Latin word for ship, *navis*. Even slipper or boat shells can remind us that we

would have tough sailing through our lives
without the safety of our church family.

*God has put all things under the power of
Christ, and for the good of the church
[God] has made him the head of everything.
The church is Christ's body
and is filled with Christ who completely
fills everything.*

Ephesians 1:22–23

**Christ, you established the church, and
through that church our relationship with
God is enriched. Thank you. Amen.**

~ of sea urchins
and opportunities

One of the most beautiful shells I know is that
of the sea urchin. It is very fragile and easily
broken. The first time I saw sea urchins washed
up on shore, I walked around picking up the
lavender colored shells with their intricate
design of holes and bumps. However, not being knowledgeable about the shell, I overlooked several prizes as I searched for what I
thought was the more important shell. In fact,
I even crushed several sea urchins that still had
their spines attached because they were cam-
ouflaged with pieces of broken shells.

The sea urchin has spines attached to the
bumps on the shell. The animal maneuvers
the spines backward and forward by using
muscles of the thin skin that covers the shell.
This movement of the spines allows the sea
urchin to progress across the floor of the sea.
The spines are also used to hold rocks and

shells above itself, providing a protective camouflage. The weight of the rocks and shells may also act as ballast during tides and strong currents.

If I overlooked the prize sea urchins because of ignorance, how many other prizes have I overlooked out of ignorance? Have I missed some great truths by keeping my life so busy that I don't have time to take part in a Bible study? Have I missed an enriching friendship or an opportunity for service? And how many personalities have I crushed because I've been so centered on myself that I have passed right by without speaking?

In issues of the law, it is understood that ignorance is not acceptable as an excuse for unlawful action. We are expected to learn the law and to be accountable to it.

The same is true with our actions as Christians. Too often we look for the prize of a lovely stained glass window or new choir robes and walk right by opportunities for service claim-

ing that we didn't see them. We must overcome our ignorance and discover ways to be
in service to others.

*My friends, you were chosen to be free.
So don't use your freedom as an excuse
to do anything you want.
Use it as an opportunity to serve
each other with love.*

Galatians 5:13

**Open my eyes, Lord, that I may see the
opportunities around me.
Help me to recognize those in need
and to choose freely to serve. Amen.**

~ of moon shells and mission

There's nothing more soothing and serene than rubbing one's finger over the smooth surface of a perfect moon shell (sometimes called a shark's or cat's eye). Perhaps this is the satisfaction that a young child experiences by rubbing the satin binding of a favorite blanket. This shell may be called a moon shell because in the midst of a light violet, sky-like surface, there is a raised circle which looks like a full moon.

From that moon-shaped center everything spirals out. Or is it that everything spirals inward, toward the center? It all depends on your perspective. It could be spiraling outward or inward.

Whether inward or outward, the moon shell has a message for us. We must seek God and spiral God's love into the very center or heart of ourselves. Unless we draw that love into us, we cannot share it with others.

On the other hand, we cannot close the trap door and keep the love to ourselves. God's love is such that when we really experience it, then we must share it with others. That is how we spiral outward, forever revealing God's love to the world. No matter how insignificant it is, when done in the service of God it is as if we were doing it for Christ himself.

Such a powerful mission we have, and such joy in receiving and carrying it out!

The king will answer,
"Whenever you did it for any of my people,
no matter how unimportant they seemed,
you did it for me."

Matthew 25:40

Help me, Lord, to draw your love
into myself so that I may then
move outward and
share your love with others. Amen.

~ of a baby's ear and a human heart

Half hidden in sand, I found a baby's ear. No, it was not the ear of a human baby, but a shell called the baby's ear. This shell is a type of moon snail, but much easier to overlook because of its plain white coloration. It may be mistaken for a common shell that has faded in the sun.

This delicate shell also spirals, but the opening of the spiral is so wide that you can look inside to the very center of the shell. There is nothing to hide in a baby's ear!

Much like the baby's ear, we should have nothing to hide from God.

God knows the true center of our beings and can see through the openings of our shells, right into our hearts and into our souls.

Young children often have difficulty understanding what we mean when we refer to our "soul." Likewise, they have difficulty with our abstract concept of the heart. One of my favorite ways to help children connect with the soul is to play a game. I touch different parts of the body, such as an arm, a leg, or their head, asking, "Is this the Really, Really You?" Usually, the answer is an emphatic "No!" Then we talk about the part of themselves that makes them laugh when they are happy, and cry when they are sad. "*That* is the Really Really You," I say, " the part we call the soul or the heart."

Like the open-ended baby's ear shell, when we are open and allow God to know what is in our heart, then we will burst out in excitement in sharing God with the world.

Look deep into my heart, God,
and find out everything I am thinking.
Don't let me follow evil ways, but lead me in
the way that time has proven true.

Psalm 139:23–24

I want to be open to the very center of my
being, God, so that you may spread your
love in and through me. Amen.

~ of fossils and days of old

The children bubbled with excitement over the upcoming Shell Fair. This was an annual affair that started well over 50 years ago in the homes and modest lodges that dotted the coast. At that time, shells were not only plentiful, but a favorite pastime for vacationers and residents alike. Now, I had been to many a county fair, particularly in South Dakota where there were as many food, sewing, craft, cattle, and gardening categories of competition as there were residents in the sparsely populated county. But I could not see how there could be much diversity in a fair that was devoted totally to shells. I was in for a new experience.

One of the boys in our church confided to me about the shell display that he was going to enter in the competition. He told me that he had collected his shells for competition and hadn't gone to the seashore for a single one of them. I accused him of visiting the local shell shop, but he assured me that he had found every one of them.

When the week arrived, I set aside an afternoon with anticipation. Many of the children had been schooled in their knowledge of the shells, and they staffed a display of live shells, explaining the environment and lifestyles of each type. There were enough shells at the fair to fill the local community center and spill onto the grounds. There were categories for every type of shell, plus competition for various crafts and artwork that used shells.

My young friend found me and proudly led me to his display. It sported a large blue ribbon. In his case was a large variety of chalky white shells, some I recognized and some I'd never seen before. The written information on his display explained that every one of his shells had been found in his driveway at home. The driveways on that island are not the usual slab of cement, but excavation fill, much of it shell. These were fossils of shells that had been covered by layers of sand as the beaches drifted and changed over the centuries.

We looked at the collection and speculated what might have been happening at the time the shells were alive. Might it have been the year that Christ was born? Or might it have been during the 40 years that the Hebrews wandered the deserts? Might the shells have been deposited at the time Abraham decided to follow God's call and move his family from Ur to a new land?

It's exciting to look at something that is literally "as old as the hills" and realize that God is the same now as then. Oh yes, many of our ideas about God have changed as we've grown in our understanding. But God is faithful and steady, always constant over the ages.

The name of the LORD will be remembered forever, and he will be famous for all time to come.

Psalm 135:13

God of the ages, I worship you today as they did long ago when the fossils were laid down. May I grow in my understanding of you even as I grow in years. Amen.

~ of marine worms
and spiritual food

When we think of beaches, we usually visualize wide stretches of sand with palm trees swaying and waves gently lapping on the shore. However, this is not the case after a storm at sea. On those days, the beach can be a mess of all sorts of things thrown up from the ocean depths and littered across the sand. On just such a day, I began my walk up the beach, at first stepping over the seaweed.

Seaweed was nothing unusual to me, but I had seldom taken the time to really look at it. I would usually give it a kick to see if any good shells were hidden underneath, but I seldom even put out the effort to bend down and pick it up. However, on this day I was consciously hunting for hidden treasures, and so I decided to take a closer look at it.

I picked up a handful of turtle grass, a type of seaweed, and began lifting the leaves. There

I found small white spots that I later learned were actually tiny marine spiral worms. They looked very much like miniature snails. Although this marine worm is not an actual shell, the small animal secretes an outer covering that appears to be a seashell, made of similar material. The marine worms attach themselves to the grass and live by filtering food from the water. Their attachment does not injure the grass. In fact, the grass is only a host to the animal.

In reflecting on this, I wonder if we sometimes look at the Bible as a source of food, when actually it should be the host that supports us as we draw our nourishment from God. It is our reference point. It keeps us in position, stabilized, and available. But the words printed in the Bible are no more than vehicles through which God speaks. We can memorize Bible verses forward and backward and we can speak all sorts of religious language, but unless we personally know God, reciting the

verses and speaking the language can be like
a noisy gong or a clanging cymbal.

*What if I could speak all languages
of humans and of angels?
If I did not love others,
I would be nothing more than a
noisy gong or a clanging cymbal.*

1 Corinthians 13:1

*God, I do want to know you better. Help me
to go beyond simply speaking religious
language so that I am accepted by church
leaders, beyond even the words of the Bible.
I yearn to come to you personally. Amen.*

~ of flashlights and faith lights

There are two different types of nighttime walks on the beach. We may walk simply to enjoy the experience of the beach at night, or we may walk looking for something specific. With the former, there is no need to have a light, but with the latter there is no need to walk unless we do have a light.

The psalmist understood the need for a light when searching. He wrote of God's Word as a lamp to light the way. I teach a weekly Bible study each year that lasts for nine months. Many of the people in the Bible study have grown up in a church and have attended some sort of Sunday school or other learning experience in the church. They are familiar with the Bible, its stories, and its principal teachings. But for most of these folks, this intensive study is the first time they have put all the parts of the Bible together into a comprehensive whole, and then stepped into the Bible themselves in order to become part of the age-old search for God.

And what an illumined world they enter through the words of the Bible! Suddenly they see themselves as an extension of a great heritage. They become excited over their connection, seeing their life and talents as a witness – in a long line of witnesses to God's truth. The Word has lit their way to seeing a purpose in their lives and a direction for their walk.

*Your word is a lamp that gives light
wherever I walk.*

Psalm 119:105

*I have walked in darkness, Lord,
sometimes simply because I felt I had
no other place to go, and sometimes
really searching for you. Today I will
replace the batteries in my flashlight by
looking for the light in your Word. Amen.*

~ of banks of shells
and the joy of the moment

Have you ever imagined yourself having so much of something you really value that you could afford to throw it into the air with joy? I've never seen this sort of fantasy actually pictured except with money, but in reality the money itself is of no more value than shells, colorful pebbles, or cancelled stamps.

I have a friend who thoroughly enjoys collecting stamps. He not only collects them for himself, but for friends around the world with whom he exchanges them. I cut every stamp I receive from its envelope, and each time I see my friend I give him a new supply. He then sits on the floor and spreads the stamps all around him, sorting them into piles, one for one friend and one for another. He has even involved his grandchildren in the experience, creating a bonding experience that they anticipate with excitement.

This was just the sort of joy that I experienced the first time I saw a large bank of shells. All my life I had enjoyed combing the beaches looking for shells. But most of the beaches I frequented had such heavy surf that the shells were all battered to pieces before they reached shore. When I first walked out on this beach I stood in awe over the banks of shells, a true feast to the eyes. I must admit that I have never actually thrown shells into the air. I might destroy them in my joy! But my family can testify that I have spent many an enjoyable hour, sitting among piles of shells, running my hands through God's gifts from the sea. If I come away with one prize miniature shell, I consider my day a success. Carefully, I take it home and put it into a glass dish that holds other such treasures.

My first trip to a butterfly atrium gave me the same sort of joy. I did not have to own the butterflies or even to take a picture of them or take them home to find the joy. There was a spiritual connection with God's creation when I simply stood still and watched them move about me, sometimes even lighting on my shoulder or in my hair. I was transported out of reality and into the center of God's creative power. Time was of no essence. I was lost in the present.

Such experiences of joy cannot come from mounds of money. They cannot even come from "climbing the corporate ladder." They come from God and are experiences through the soul.

Come and see the fearsome things
our God has done!

Psalm 66:5

My God, you are fearsome, or awesome!
You come to us in unexpected ways.
Such time with you is of more worth
than all the money in the world. Amen.

~ of sand dollars and symbols

We were on a beach that was new to us. In fact, we weren't even prepared for serious beach bumming! After finishing our simple lunch fare, we left our things on the picnic table and pulled off our shoes and rolled up our pants for a walk along the shore.

We were in luck! There were sand dollars washed up on the shore all along the water line. Laughing and splashing through the waters, we felt like kids out of school. We picked up sand dollars as we wandered farther and farther. When our pockets and hands were full, we turned to go back to our table, only to discover that we had crossed a shallow inlet which now was a small river with the rising tide. If we returned the way we came, we would have to swim with our clothes on and leave our sand dollars behind! There was a road ahead of us, and we remembered from the map of the island that it would cross the little river and connect with the main road, which would lead us back to the beach where we had left our shoes. Clutching our sand dollars, we began the long trek. It was pretty slow going. If we walked on the roadway, the hot pavement blistered our feet, but along the right-of-way we discovered sandspurs. Thankfully, a local resident recognized our dilemma and stopped to give us a ride.

When we returned to our lodging, we learned more about the sand dollars that had led us on our foolish venture. The shell is literally filled with Christian symbols. The top of the shell has an outline of the Easter Lily with a five pointed star in the center. There are five oval openings which might represent the four nail holes and the one spear hole in Christ's body. Another flower, the poinsettia, is outlined on bottom of the shell. And when the shell is broken, the five teeth of the sand dollar make a star shape. When these teeth are pulled apart, each one appears in the shape of a dove. The dove is not only a symbol for peace, but it reminds us of Jesus' baptism.

We saved our sand dollars and were able to share them and their symbols with others on special occasions.

While everyone else was being baptized, Jesus himself was baptized. Then as he prayed, the sky opened up, and the Holy Spirit came down upon him in the form of a dove. A voice from heaven said, "You are my own dear Son, and I am pleased with you."

Luke 3:21–22

Often symbols help me to remember you,
Lord. You are obvious **everywhere**
if we will only remain alert.
Give me the eyes to see
and the heart to understand. Amen.

Sandcastles
Dreaming Dreams

When I see a sandcastle on the beach, I realize
that someone has had a plan. Someone set out
to accomplish something, even if the
sandcastle is partially washed away by the
tide. We can never achieve anything unless we
begin.

~ of sandcastles and petrified wood

One of my favorite activities at the beach is building sandcastles. I recall the vacation when there were only adults in our party, and the adults did not share my need to build sandcastles.

Why is it that we adults don't build sandcastles? We think that we must have a child with us to justify playing in the sand. Is it the temporal nature of sandcastles that bothers us? Do we believe that any activity that is not permanent is unworthy of participation by adults? Yet we appreciate the effort it takes to create an elaborate wedding cake, knowing it will be eaten in a few hours. Or we will take a book to the beach to read, and probably forget the contents by the end of our vacation. There's absolutely no permanence in a card game or a game of golf, but we certainly enjoy these adult activities. Maybe this is an area where Jesus would tell us that we must become like children and relish in building sandcastles for the pure joy of it.

On this particular day at the beach, my need to build sandcastles became so strong that I began to build one alone. When some children stopped to see what I was doing I invited them to join me. We put sand and water in a pail and then began taking handfuls of the wet sand, dribbling it in peaks and valleys until we had a magnificent sandcastle, complete with courtyards and buttresses. We knew that the high tide would wash our sandcastle away, but for that day it was real. And it would forever be a part of our memory. Had we wanted it to last forever, we would have built it of something more solid.

In contrast to sandcastles on a tide-washed beach, there is a park in the small town of Lemmon, South Dakota, where structures were built from petrified wood. During the depression of the '30s, a caring man helped to improve the self-esteem of jobless people by employing them to build these structures.

The shape of these permanent structures reminds me very much of sandcastles, with their peaked tops and wider bases. But there are several differences. The petrified wood park is located far from any high tides or flood potential. There isn't much danger of these castles being swept away by water. The stone castles are also built of very durable rocks, and these are cemented into place permanently. As the generations have passed since the building of the park, some people have appreciated the structures and others have thought them an eyesore. But barring the use of major demolition equipment, there is no way that these structures will be changed. The design is literally set in stone!

Our dreams are something like that. We may find that our dreams fall apart if they are not built on solid ground or a firm foundation of confidence in God. When we build at random and don't do the necessary ground-work, then there is no permanence. On the other hand, we don't want our dreams to be so solidly cemented that when circumstances change and we need to adjust them, we come up against a stone wall, so to speak. Our dreams and plans for the future are actually not our own. They are God's dreams. May we seek God's wisdom, not only to base them on a solid foundation, but also to build some flexibility into the design.

Anyone who hears my teachings and doesn't obey them is like a foolish person who built a house on sand. The rain poured down, the rivers flooded, and the winds blew and beat against that house. Finally, it fell with a crash.

Matthew 7:26–27

Give my dreams the strength of stone, God, and the flexibility of sand. Amen.

~ of sea horses and God's gifts

One of my earliest fascinations with the ocean was with sea horses. In fact, I'm not sure that I realized the animal actually lived in the sea. I know that I had no idea what it might look like when it was alive, because I recall my disbelief when I saw a live sea horse for the first time. The sharp ridges that I liked so well were covered by leather-like skin. The shape was similar, but could this be the same animal?

I have a friend who recently discovered the joy of living a God-centered life. He told me of the many people with whom he worked who asked him, "What's made you so different? Something has changed your life."

It's interesting how other people can recognize the difference when we allow Christ to change our lives. Could we actually be the same persons? God sees the delicate framework on the inside of ourselves from the very beginning, even when we have covered it with a thick leathery skin. God knows the potential, whether we recognize it or not.

I was also surprised when I learned that the female sea horse deposits her eggs in the pouch of the male sea horse. The male incubates the eggs, and eventually hundreds of tiny animals emerge. I wonder if we can learn from this arrangement in God's plan about the maternal opportunities available for both males and females.

Another interesting thing I learned about the sea horse is its lack of power as a swimmer. Since God did not give the sea horse the gift of powerful fins, God gave it the gift of a strong tail. With this tail, the sea horse can grasp underwater plants and protect itself from aimless movements that ocean currents may cause.

Other creatures of the sea have different protective devices as gifts from God. It may be a camouflage of color or a sharp stinging tail. Or it may be venom to stun predators, or the strength to pull away.

The sea's inhabitants have learned to recognize the gifts that God gave them and to use them as God planned. Since human gifts are so varied, we sometimes think that we aren't important if we don't have the specific gifts that are obvious in other people. However, we need to realize that even if we lack obvious gifts like the tarpon's strength for swimming, God has given each of us the gifts we need to complete the plan God has for us.

*God has also given each of us
different gifts to use.*

Romans 12:6

Help me, God, to recognize the gifts you have given me and to use them to follow your calling for my life. Amen.

~ of sandcastles and relationships

I seldom take a beach trip but that I find at least one sandcastle dissolved by a rising tide or demolished by the feet of a human or an animal. Sometimes there will be a second and a third sandcastle, each built a little further back from the water's edge. Granted, we expect sandcastles to be temporary, to be washed away by the tides. When we've finished building them, we don't throw up a fence to keep animals or other people from ruining them.

Unfortunately, all too often we look at relationships in the same way. We develop a relationship simply for the superficial joy, or for some temporary benefit. Then we sit back and say, "Well that's finished," and discard our building tools.

Years ago I read a definition of friendship that used three categories: intimate, close, and casual. Intimate friends are few and far between. We may have only a few intimate relationships in our lifetime. Close friends enjoy many things in common. They thrive on the give-and-take of conversations about mutual interests. They share excitement and joys as well as sorrows that come their way. Casual friends often develop in neighborhood locations, among business associates, and through other friends.

With nurture and care, any of these relationships can move from one form of friendship into the next. But our problem comes when we try to force the casual or close relationship into an intimate relationship without first laying a firm foundation on the bedrock of our souls. Then, each time something threatens the relationship like the wash from an incoming tide, we abandon it and move on to build another, hoping to avoid any danger.

Such relationships, like sandcastles, are lovely on the outside but without a firm foundation. God created us to be in relationship with other persons and we feel out of sorts when that doesn't happen. As a result, we may build first one sandcastle relationship and then another, but never take the time or energy to dig deep and sink the foundations of the relationship into a bedrock of spiritual life. Consequently, when heavy winds and high tides threaten the relationship, it falls. Then we blame it on the exterior winds and tides, instead of recognizing that the problem lies in our lack of foundation in God.

*May God bless you with [God's] love
and may the Holy Spirit join all your
hearts together.*

2 Corinthians 13:13b

You made us to be in relationship with one another, my God. Guide me as I try to build those relationships on firm foundations that will become dreams come true. Amen.

~ of boulders and sunrise

I rose early and slipped into a robe. I had slept late other mornings of this vacation, but this morning I was determined to see the sunrise on the beach. With a cup of tea in hand, I slipped out on the balcony of our rented condo and sat in the comfortable chair. The sky was beginning to lighten, and there was a hint of color.

I had not even brought a pad and pen because I was simply going to sit – basking in the delight of God's world as the new day dawned, sipping my tea and watching, waiting for the bright orange ball to pop over the horizon. As my eyes wandered down the beach I noticed a large boulder. In the early light, the shadows played on the rock giving it a distinct shape. I puzzled over the shape, trying to see different images in it. However, as it became lighter, I gave up trying to see an image in it – I could see nothing more than a boulder.

Suddenly I realized that the sun was above the horizon and I hadn't even seen it rise. I had focused my eyes on something else, on the boulder down the beach, and had missed the sunrise. Why had I let my eyes wander?

All too often we let obstacles block us from the very thing we're seeking. Or they may simply distract us. Either way, obstacles are what we see when we take our eyes off the goal. I would have to wait for another morning to see the sun rise over the sea. But there will be other opportunities, and I will keep reaching toward my goal.

I have not yet reached my goal,
and I am not perfect. But Christ has taken
hold of me. So I keep on running and
struggling to take hold of the prize.

Philippians 3:13

Help me, O God, to ignore the boulders
and keep my eyes on the goal. Amen.

~ of conch shells and rituals

One of the prized possessions in our home is an old conch shell with a hole cut in one end. No one seems to know just how it came into my husband's family, because all of his family lived in northern Europe or the Midwest of the United States, far from the native seas of the conch. The shell was used as a horn to call the threshers in from the field for dinner.

When I lived in Key West as a teenager, I learned that the early inhabitants of the area blew into large conch shells to communicate. They also used the shells in their religious rituals. Many peoples have created horns from something common to their area in order communicate or to enhance their religious rituals. Flutes were made from reeds, and drums from hollowed out tree trunks. Among people who raised sheep, a ram's horn was used, and the coastal peoples blew into shells. Whatever they found became useful in their rituals. It was important to communicate with each other and to communicate with God.

Sometimes we become stuck on a certain method of communication with God. Because our religious parents used a certain method of worship, we feel that there is no other way to make contact with God. Such an attitude blocks many creative ways to experience God. Only by stretching our dreams can we fully experience God.

Sing a new song to the LORD! Everyone on this earth, sing praises to the LORD, sing and praise [God's] name.

Psalm 96:1

There are many ways to communicate with you, O Lord. Help me to reach for new opportunities. Amen.